Storybuilding

Resource Books for Teachers
series editor Alan Maley

Storybuilding

Jane Spiro

OXFORD
UNIVERSITY PRESS

OXFORD

UNIVERSITY PRESS

Great Clarendon Street, Oxford OX2 6DP

Oxford University Press is a department of the University of Oxford.
It furthers the University's objective of excellence in research, scholarship,
and education by publishing worldwide in

Oxford New York

Auckland Cape Town Dar es Salaam Hong Kong Karachi
Kuala Lumpur Madrid Melbourne Mexico City Nairobi
New Delhi Shanghai Taipei Toronto

With offices in

Argentina Austria Brazil Chile Czech Republic France Greece
Guatemala Hungary Italy Japan Poland Portugal Singapore
South Korea Switzerland Thailand Turkey Ukraine Vietnam

OXFORD and OXFORD ENGLISH are registered trade marks of
Oxford University Press in the UK and in certain other countries

ISBN-13: 987 019 4421935
ISBN-10: 0 19 442193 7

Printed in China

Acknowledgements

The activities in this book were developed with language learners, teachers, storytellers, and trainee storytellers in the following places and with the following classes:

Bedford College of Higher Education, UK
Primary Language Centres in Bedford, UK
British Council Literature workshop, Velke Mezirici, Czech Republic
Klubschule Migros, St. Gallen, Switzerland
ETAS St. Gallen, Aachen and Zurich, Switzerland
Volkshochschule Murten and Weinfelden, Switzerland
University of Nottingham Department of English Studies, Nottingham UK
British Council workshops in Pondicherry, Bangalore, Coimbatore, Chidambaran, India
British Council workshops in Tokyo and Fujinomiya, Japan
British Council Cairo, Egypt
Janus Pannonius University, Pécs, Hungary
British Council Conference, Naples, Italy
British Council PRINCE project workshops in Gdansk, Torun and Vigry, Poland
Creative English class at the College of St. Mark and St. John 1998
Malaysian B.Ed. teachers at the College of St. Mark and St. John 1993 to 2000
Mexican B.Phil. Ed. students in Mexicali and Ensenada, Mexico
Park Primary School, Plymouth, UK
Totnes School of English, Totnes, Devon, UK
IATEFL SIG workshops: London, UK
IATEFL conferences: Edinburgh, Scotland and Dublin, Ireland
International Projects Centre (IPC) Exeter
Ministry of Education Stage 3 Workshop for Literature teachers, Valbonne, France 2002
Beijing Foreign Studies University, Beijing, China 2002
The novel writers' circle, Plymouth 1997, Exeter 2003
Swedish teachers with Utbildingsstaden in Oxford, UK 2001 to 2004
Tammi Finnish teachers in Helsinki, Finland 2004
The Finding Voices class: Oxford Brookes University 2001/2004
The Language through Literature class: Oxford Brookes University 2004/2005
Damai Laut, Malaysia and MICELT, Melaka, Malaysia 2005

Thanks to many who set up events for me to tell, write, and develop stories with teachers and students:

Roselle Angwin, Peter Holland, Jean Rudiger, Amos Paran, Ron Carter, Cathy Pickles, Robert Bellarmine, Tracey Gilpin, Sue Parker, Liz Robbins, Katy Salisbury, Cecilia Augutis, Bengt Andersson, Lesley Hayman, Martin Bates, Rob Pope, Chrissie Mortimer, John McRae, Antoinette Moses, Jaya Mukundan

The stories in this book are my own tellings or retellings, unless otherwise stated. The sparks for these stories come from:

Inca, American Indian, Swedish, Russian, Celtic, Arabic, African and Chinese folktales and myths

FAVOURITE STORIES
Frank O'Connor: 'My Oedipus Complex',
John Lanchester: *The Debt to Pleasure*,
Alphonse Daudet: *Lettres de mon moulin*,
Raymond Carver: 'Elephant'.

POEM Robert Browning: *The Pied Piper of Hamelin*,
OPERA PLOT Donizetti's *L'Elisir d'Amore*
JOKES Yiddish, Arabic, on the grapevine

STORIES DEVELOPED WITH AND IN CLASSES
Family stories: The city monkeys (Uncle Norman's story)
Local stories: The king's dinner (King Charles I in Totnes)
Teacher and student stories: Tigers and tapping ghosts, Inderjit and Sumi
Friends' stories: Eli's story

MY OWN STORIES
The Place of the Lotus: originally published with Thomas Nelson: reissued by Edward Arnold, 1990
The Twin Chariot: originally published with Thomas Nelson: reissued by Edward Arnold, 1990
Cyberbuddies: serialised by Cornelsen Verlag online
The International Visitors: serialized by Cornelsen Verlag online
Nothing I Touch Stands Still: a novel. Crucible Press, 2002
'Travelling Light' in *London Tales* ELI Recanati
'The Man Upstairs' in *A Twist in the Tale* ELI Recanati

Special thanks to my husband John Daniel, for brainstorming plot types throughout a summer holiday in Italy, and for being a true partner in storymaking.

Illustrations by Philip Burrows

Contents

Index

The author and series editor

Jane Spiro is Head of Applied Linguistics and Principal Lecturer at Oxford Brookes University, and course manager of the MA in ELT for in-service teachers. She teaches and manages modules at MA and BA level related to teacher development, reflective teaching, language/literature interface, second and first language writing, testing and evaluation, and storytelling. She has taught language learners and teachers from beginner to MA level in schools and colleges worldwide, including Belgium, Switzerland, Hungary, Poland, India, Mexico, and China. Her interests include creative writing and literature in the language classroom, test writing and materials writing for teachers, teacher development and the role of teacher narratives. She was co-editor of the journal *Reading in a Foreign Language* until 2001. She has also been a presenter and writer of interfaith programmes for Carlton and West Country TV, and has published plays, stories, and poems, both in educational and mainstream settings. In 2002 she published her first novel, *Nothing I Touch Stands Still* (Crucible Press), and is the author of *Creative Poetry Writing* in the Resource Books for Teachers series.

Alan Maley worked for The British Council from 1962 to 1988, serving as English Language Officer in Yugoslavia, Ghana, Italy, France, and China, and as Regional Representative in South India (Madras). From 1988 to 1993 he was Director-General of the Bell Educational Trust, Cambridge. From 1993 to 1998 he was Senior Fellow in the Department of English Language and Literature of the National University of Singapore, and from 1998 to 2002 he was Director of the graduate programme at Assumption University, Bangkok. He is currently a freelance consultant. Among his publications are *Literature*, in this series, *Beyond Words*, *Sounds Interesting*, *Sounds Intriguing*, *Words*, *Variations on a Theme*, and *Drama Techniques in Language Learning* (all with Alan Duff), *The Mind's Eye* (with Françoise Grellet and Alan Duff), *Learning to Listen* and *Poem into Poem* (with Sandra Moulding), *Short and Sweet*, and *The English Teacher's Voice*.

Foreword

In recent years there has been a resurgence of interest in 'story', both in general, and, more specifically, related to the application of storytelling to ELT. The value of stories to humankind is well-attested. Stories help us to understand who we are, to make sense of the confusing swirl of everyday life, to digest and transform our experiences. They can also serve to develop reflection and critical thinking. Within ELT, stories help promote motivation (everyone loves a good story!), and offer a rich array of spin-off activities to develop language proficiency, especially fluency, and a creative, risk-taking relationship with the language.

There have been a number of groundbreaking books in the area of storytelling, starting as long ago as 1983 with Morgan and Rinvolucri's pioneering *Once Upon a Time*. Andrew Wright's two books in this series, *Storytelling with Children* and *Creating Stories with Children*, have extended the use of story to the field of Young Learners. So what is the unique contribution of this new book? It is the first comprehensive attempt to engage teenage and adult learners in the activity of creating and writing their own stories. No other manual of activities for foreign-language learners exists in this area. It is absolutely unique.

The book offers a carefully structured series of activities which, in a non-threatening way, guides the learners to write their own stories. It effortlessly overcomes the frequently voiced objections to this kind of work (stories are too childish for adult learners, 'but I'm not a creative person', etc.). The activities are based on the author's long-term practical experience with using creative story writing in many parts of the world, both in workshops and in regular classroom teaching. All the activities have been carefully trialled.

The book is a fine companion volume to *Creative Poetry Writing* by the same author. Together they offer a goldmine of stimulating yet practical activities for the busy, but enterprising teacher. They will not disappoint.

Alan Maley

Introduction

Why was this book written?

Stories are very much part of our lives as adults as well as children. We hear stories every day on the news, read them in the newspaper, exchange them with friends as jokes, anecdotes, rumours, stories overheard or ways of sharing confidences. We collect stories we consider funny, surprising or shocking, and which throw light on what is happening in the world and our views about this. It is one way we exchange information, both about events that have really happened, and those that have been imagined.

Similarly, there seem to be certain universals about what makes a story work well. Soap operas, stereotype jokes, cult heroes, and the lives of media personalities, all become part of the shared language of modern life, just as nursery tales are shared language between parent and child. We are great consumers of 'story', and storytelling is a sub-skill of social life. The 'storytelling circles' of ancient tradition exist now as groups of friends in a cafe sharing jokes, colleagues telling stories about the boss during the coffee break, or a family sitting round the television watching a soap opera.

Yet the scope of story is even broader than this. What is the connection, for example, between the friends sharing confidences about their lives on a mobile phone, and the written stories that we see in bookshop windows, which may win literary prizes and make their authors millionaires? The first kind of 'story' is informal, spontaneous, and oral; it is developed by two or more people in conversation; and it relates closely to their everyday lives and to shared understandings within it. The second kind of story, in contrast, is probably structured with great care and formality, has taken months or years to refine, and is the voice of one specific author made public and accessible to as many readers as possible. Yet both have the same quality. They make us feel: *I am interested in this story; I want to know what happens next.* Stories make us read or listen on, because through them we experience suspense or surprise, excitement, fear and its resolution, empathy with main characters, insights into our own lives and beliefs, the fantastic or the impossible. Stories, both oral and literary, have combinations of some or all of these elements.

This book will attempt to offer the learner skills for both kinds of story. On the one hand, the activities will invite them to build stories with partners, sharing ideas informally and guiding them towards storytelling skills such as using the voice to 'play all the parts', using mime, music, and props, inviting audience participation, and improvising (Chapter 9). On the other hand, the activities will help learners to commit their ideas to writing, editing, and correcting their own work, and polishing it for written 'publication' (Chapter 10). It will also look at the kind of ingredients that both stories share: the development of character, dialogue and description, plot, settings and situations, openings and closures.

This book was written to reflect this broad scope of 'story', and the universal qualities that make them shared and enjoyed by people of all ages, cultures and backgrounds.

Storytelling and the learner

How can stories develop students' language skills?

Stories practise all kinds of language. In a good story, we need to describe places and people, write dialogues using different voices, make things happen, show the results and causes of things; we can discuss and argue; we can use parts of letters or diaries. Some writers even include recipes and menus in their novels.

The activities in this book will show how a story can be used in all the following ways:

- to practise both speaking and writing skills in a context which is deeply engaging and personalized
- to encourage group sharing, team-building, and co-operative text-making
- as opportunities to develop oral fluency and confidence
- for specific language practice of tenses, descriptive adjectives, reporting verbs, and punctuation for direct speech
- for specific language practice of functions such as giving advice, describing, and instructing
- for development of extensive writing that includes narrative, description, dialogue, and character development
- to provide an incentive for learners to write, edit, and reformulate their writing so it can be shared with others
- to prepare students for the written narrative components of exams such as First Certificate, Proficiency, and IELTS
- to encourage learners to read more appreciatively, and to understand the processes of story writing for themselves.

Much can be done with the outcomes of story activities:

- students can share stories orally in class
- the stories can be developed into short sketches or pieces of 'mini-theatre'
- stories can be written during the lesson, then displayed around the walls

- stories can be edited and corrected after the lesson, typed up and included in a class collection
- stories from one class can be used as readings for another class
- students can explain why they wrote a story, or what they would like readers/listeners to notice about their story.

How can stories develop students' learning skills?

At the first level, storytelling can develop the memory; we retell stories we have just heard, we remember sequences of events, names of characters, and even whole 'chunks' of language, such as 'Grandma, what big ears/eyes/teeth you have!' But in retelling, we also summarize, edit, and develop; we add a detail here, a conversation there. Having told our story, we evaluate its success, recall the timing or wording that made our audience laugh, exaggerate a character to make him/her funnier or more frightening, revise the punch line so we make our point more clearly. The building blocks of story can help us—character, plot, settings—but these alone are not enough to make a story work. We need to be clear about what we want to say, why, how, and for whom, and to work on making the story in our head match as closely as possible the story that is read or listened to.

These broad skills and abilities transfer to all subject disciplines, and to writing in all contexts, both formal and informal. Academic writers, for example, will need to ask the same questions as storywriters: have I adapted my writing to match my audience? Have I made my point clear? Have I marked clearly the stages in my narrative so the reader recognizes beginnings, endings, and key moves in between? Is the reader motivated to read on?

So to prepare the ground well as a storyteller is to give your students many learning opportunities that will help them both inside and outside the language classroom. A good writer of stories is a good writer; a good storyteller is a skilled and confident speaker.

Myths about stories: what teachers and learners say about stories

Adults like to talk about the real world. Stories are too childish for adult learners.

The fact is, stories **are** about the real world. They draw on, and remind us of, our memories, our friends and relations, places we have lived in and visited.

At the same time, stories are playful. They remind adult learners of the kind of 'play' they enjoyed as children: making up larger-than-life characters, giving them strange names, dropping them into fantasy worlds, imagining extraordinary scientific inventions. Yet even these often reflect interestingly on the 'real' world. Looking at them again, as adult readers and story-writers, we might find that in fact our fantastic world on the moon is rather like the one on earth, and the extraterrestrial creatures we have invented are rather like the people we meet every day, or the ones we see on television.

In fact, sometimes we can think about real life more clearly by keeping a certain distance from it, by allowing ourselves to follow ideas or dreams, rather than being hooked to the details of real life. Fables and myths are fantastical and often surreal, but they can often answer questions about the real world better than realistic stories do.

But I am not imaginative. How can I possibly write a story?

Stories come from many places. We do not need to be imaginative geniuses to find sources of story around us. There are:

- stories which are retellings of others we know well, dropped into a different context, or with changed characters or settings
- stories based on snippets of news or snatches of information overheard on the radio
- stories based on stories we overhear, moments in a conversation overheard at a bus-stop, or on the train
- stories based on brief meetings and encounters with people that make us wonder how they got to be the way they are
- stories based on information we have researched about a person or a place
- stories based on answers to problems
- stories which are shared orally, passed on by word of mouth from person to person and parent to child
- stories that become local 'myths' simply because they are told so often, and frequently with interesting variations and exaggerations. Often no one knows where these stories began or whether they are fact or fiction
- stories that cover huge amounts of time, such as three generations of a family
- stories that are tiny, and begin and end in 50 words.

This book will give learners opportunities to experiment with all these story types, and to choose the ones that suit them best.

Can people be taught to tell a story?

Yes. There are ways in which even the best storytellers need to practise and refine their craft. We can practise in just the same way:

- making the characters in our story 'rounded' and realistic (Chapter 3)
- choosing details to make a story come alive (Chapter 4)
- planning plots where 'something happens' (Chapter 5)
- using the ingredients of good stories to help us with our own (throughout)
- developing our vocabulary so it describes what we want to say more precisely (throughout)

- editing our story for ideas, stylistic variety, and accuracy (Chapter 10).

This book will work with activities that all learners can try for themselves. Many of them can be used at pre-intermediate level, and require no special knowledge, technical language, or experience of writing.

Storytelling and you the teacher

The activities in this book can also help you to become a more confident and courageous storyteller in the classroom. Apart from being a language programme for learners, this book can also serve as storytelling training for you in your role as teacher, allowing you to collect, prepare, develop, perform, and exploit stories for use in the classroom.

Story preparation checklist for the teacher

You can also use this book as a starting point for building up a 'story bank' for constant use in the classroom. The stories here can be drawn on to fill a quiet classroom moment, for warm-ups and warm-downs, to welcome a new class, or say goodbye at the end of term. They are easy to collect, once you are aware of just how rich our world is with story potential.

- For an anecdote to become a story, a storyteller might simply need to develop the details, and use fictional names and places. The checklists in Chapter 10 can help to turn any interesting anecdote or snatched storyline into a story worth sharing.
- You could also build up a set of materials that your students can use as a basis for storytelling.
- Build up a set of photos of people and places (activity 2.6 suggests ways of using pictures and photos for storytelling).
- Note down interesting names of people and places.
- Keep a collection of student examples of names and nicknames (activity 3.1 can help you to do this).
- Build a bank of interesting newspaper headlines and articles (activity 2.2).
- Keep synopses of books and stories enjoyed by yourself and your learners in a file in the classroom, for reference and development (see 'Story Bluff', activity 8.6, which uses story synopses).
- Keep a note of interesting proverbs and sayings (see activity 2.3).

Storytelling skills for the teacher

For you to make the most of telling and writing your own stories in class, the following skills will be helpful:

Simplifying stories that are too difficult

Below are some strategies for 'grading' a story to match the level of your class:

More difficult	Less difficult
Phrasal verbs: He got on with the job of looking for the gold.	Single verbs: He looked everywhere for the gold.
Less frequently used words: They chattered away.	Commonly used words: They talked.
Complex sentences	Simple sentences
Specific words: the tulip and the hyacinth	General words: the flowers

However, evidence has shown that adults, like children, can absorb more unfamiliar words than usual if they are engaged in a story, and following its plot with interest. The context will show them, for example, that Sleeping Beauty has been pricked by the thorn of a rose, or that Cinderella has left a glass slipper behind at the ball. Simple props or 'realia' can help to illustrate key notions in a story, so that you can continue to use 'roughly tuned input' to introduce new vocabulary at key points in the story.

Using props and 'realia' to illustrate aspects of a story

A few very simple props, such as hats to denote different characters, coloured scarves to denote rain, and wind, movement of trees, can help to bring a story alive. See Chapter 9 for more ideas.

Memorizing stories

See the notes in activity 9.1 to help you choose between reading a story aloud, and memorizing it to allow for improvisation, changes, and your own language.

Storytelling and the language syllabus

The storytelling activities in this book can be used specifically to match different aspects of your language syllabus. The index shows you how you can select activities to match a range of teaching goals and programmes:

- functions
- grammar and accuracy
- punctuation
- story starting points

- story synopses
- storytelling skills and ingredients
- text types
- topics
- vocabulary
- writing skills.

How should the teacher deal with errors in stories?

What you choose to do with learner errors will depend on your goals as a teacher. For example:

- if your goal is to encourage oral fluency, you might make a note of some of the key errors that disturb comprehension, and report back on these once the storyteller has finished
- if your goal is a precise linguistic one, such as correct use of past tenses, you might ask learners to self-correct just this aspect of their work, then check the work again yourself
- if your goal is to encourage writing fluency, you might invite learners to read one another's stories to check for clarity and comprehensibility. Ask them to check with you if there are any parts that they cannot correct or improve for themselves.

How to use this book

What does each activity contain?

- Each activity includes group- or pair-work that focuses on listening and speaking: oral storytelling, followed by a writing stage with explicit guidance for teacher and learner as to areas of accuracy and skills to be developed. This means each activity can be used to practise oral skills only or can be extended into a writing task that focuses on fluency, coherence, specific vocabulary, or grammatical accuracy.
- Each activity can be developed for the purposes of group dynamic and team-building, fluency skills, or specific language skills, such as: adjectives to describe people and places, dialogue and verbs of speaking, reported speech, talking about the past and the future, functions of giving advice, describing, instructing, or explaining.
- The activities as a whole work with the key story-building features, so the learner will be able to develop a story idea in every lesson, and, across a sequence of lessons, will gain a 'toolkit' of skills for generating longer stories. These skills will include: finding starting points for stories, developing a character in a story, describing settings and situations in stories, and starting and finishing stories in different ways.
- Your learners, however, do not have to be 'storytellers' to start with. Every learner, even the ones who say, 'I have no imagination', will find there are sources of stories, and possibilities for developing them, in many places: in newspaper headlines, pictures

and photos, television stories and soap operas, conversations overheard, rumours and gossip, dreams and nightmares.

- Many activities offer examples of stories and synopses of stories used with and developed by similar learners in workshops worldwide.
- The activities can be taught progressively, leading to the 'publication' of a class anthology, or polished and edited pieces of individual work, or to oral storytelling circles in which learners, in groups or individually, develop the confidence to take the floor.
- The activities can be self-contained, and taught in any sequence, although the index offers guidance for teachers who are seeking a specific sequence based on skills development, grammar and vocabulary, and text types or functions.
- No technical equipment of any kind is required, including tape-recorders or photocopied material. The only assumption is that the teacher is able to write on a blackboard.

How is the book organized?

The book takes you on a journey, from the first story sparks to the development of characters, descriptions of their surroundings, the twists and turns of the plot, and ending with editing and performance.

Chapter 1: Story building blocks

This chapter offers an introduction to the overarching storytelling principles that inform the book as a whole, including the ingredients of stories, types of story, ways of organizing information in stories, beginnings and endings, and the connection between ideas.

Chapter 2: Sources of stories

This chapter considers a number of different starting points for stories, such as newspaper headlines, pictures, retelling familiar stories, writers' notebooks, proverbs and sayings, family stories, and stories based on local history.

Chapter 3: Story stars

Here we develop characters in stories: finding them from our own experiences, naming them, and inviting them to talk, think, search, have conversations, and wear typical items from their daily wardrobe.

Chapter 4: A sense of place

This chapter places characters in their settings. We look at places where characters are most comfortable, and where they are least comfortable, and describe the details of their environments, and the different terrains encountered on their journeys.

Chapter 5: Something happened

This chapter looks at how storytellers introduce different kinds of action in a story, such as: a journey, an arrival, a return, a loss, and a difficult choice. The chapter offers the storyteller a range of plot types from which an infinite number of further stories can be generated.

Chapter 6: Pattern stories

These are stories that work with specific language patterns, such as sequences of adverbial phrases, chants or echoes in the present simple, and refrains that function like substitution charts with minimal changes. Pattern stories are excellent for the less advanced learner, and also for the teacher who wishes to develop a specific structure in a dynamic and unusual way. The chapter works with the four sentence types—statement, command, instruction, and question—and shows how these can be the building blocks of story.

Chapter 7: Voices in stories

This chapter shows that stories do not need to be presented in a simple and linear way, using the narrative voice. We can tell a story through letters, diaries, newspaper articles, radio commentaries, and even doctors' reports, recipes, and menus. This chapter works with a single story, showing how it can be developed through a 'portfolio' of text types that give us an insight into the thinking of many different characters.

Chapter 8: Story games

Chapter Eight shows many ways in which stories can also be games and competitions, so they can be dropped into the warm-up or warm-down phases of the lesson: for example, guessing beginnings and endings, jigsaw stories, chain stories, and stories which grow smaller and bigger.

Chapter 9: Performing story

The chapter offers specific techniques for oral storytelling: memorizing and reading aloud, playing all the parts by changing voice pitch and intonation, using music props and sound effects, developing choral storytelling in which the class becomes an 'orchestra'. The techniques can be used by the teacher who wants to become more effective as a storyteller; or communicated to students so they too develop oral confidence. Most excitingly, the skills can be developed with the class as a whole, so their own stories can generate classroom theatre.

Chapter 10: Publishing stories

This final chapter offers the teacher a number of editing checklists that can be used for self-, peer-, or teacher-editing of written stories. They focus on editing for accuracy, stylistic variety, vocabulary, story ideas, and characterization. The chapter ends with an editing workshop, in which an example of a revised story is shared.

Three appendices at the end of the book include:

- a checklist of plot archetypes and characters as a resource for limitless story variations
- a glossary of terms used to describe stories
- websites and references to teaching materials, stories, and further reading for the teacher.

The index includes:

- a list of the 25 complete story synopses included in this book, which can be used as freestanding stories in the language lesson
- a list of routes through the book, showing ways to sequence the activities if you are planning a syllabus based on: writing skills, grammar and vocabulary, functions, or text types.

1
Story building blocks

What is story? One storyteller, Andrew Wright, calls stories 'descriptions of dramatic events in fiction or fact'. This is a useful definition, and leads us to more questions. How do we make events dramatic? What is the difference between fiction and fact? Do we have to choose between these two when we tell a story? What is the shape of a description? Descriptions can be linear, or circular, or repetitive, and information can be organized in all kinds of different ways to give the description a different emphasis. This chapter will look at some of these key elements and questions about a story, and will ask a few more questions on the way.

1.1 Ingredients of story: Petunia the parrot

Level Elementary and above

Time 30 minutes

Aims To look at the key ingredients of story; to consider the difference between three connected sentences and a story with development.

Procedure

1 Write the following sentences on the board. Under Variations below, there are other examples you could choose to suit your class.

Example Petunia, the parrot, sat on her eggs. She sat, and sat, and sat, and sat. Then one day there was a *peck-peck*, and a baby parrot walked out.

2 Ask your learners whether this is a story or not. Ask the class to make a choice, and give you a show of hands. How many said: 'Yes, it is?' How many said: 'No, it isn't?'

3 Ask your learners to work with someone who agreed with them to draw up a list of reasons for their decision. With elementary learners, this discussion could be done in their mother tongue. 'It is a story because …', 'It isn't a story because …'

4 After five minutes, invite the learners to share their views and collect ideas on the board under the heading 'Stories'. You'll find some in the board plan below.

Worksheet 1.1
Stories

Stories have a main character.

Something happens in a story.

There is a beginning, middle, and end (but not necessarily in that order).

Something should be difficult for the main character.

He/she should go somewhere, do something, or have a problem.

Something changes in a story.

The end is different from the beginning.

Photocopiable © Oxford University Press

5   Now ask your learners to choose one story ingredient from the list on the board. Ask them to work with a partner to add or develop this ingredient in Petunia's story, for example: 'Something should be difficult for the main character.'

Example   Petunia the parrot sat on her eggs. But they weren't her eggs at all. They belonged to the hen who lived next door.

Variation 1

Ask your learners to write three connected sentences of their own.

Sentence 1: a statement, describing a situation or a scene
Sentence 2: what happens next
Sentence 3: decide on your own third sentence.

Is this a story? Why or why not?

Variation 2

Here are two other texts you could use as starting points.

Example A   The man was building a house. He built the first layer of bricks, then the second layer, then the third, then the fourth. At last, the house was finished, so he went to sleep.

Example B   The girl with the straw hat walked through the field. Then she walked through another field, and through a gate, and over a fence, and through a hedge, and over a river. Then she sat down on a stone and took off her hat.

1.2 Types of story: tigers and tapping ghosts

Level Intermediate and above

Learners will need to have some understanding of different story types, such as science fiction, romance, or thriller. These are explained in the appendix at the end of this book.

Time 20–40 minutes

Aims To define story types and their features; to write 'blurbs' about books; to make vocabulary choices for different story types.

Preparation

Check the appendix for definitions of the story types at step 2 below.

You may wish to prepare the list of story types in advance, writing it on a hidden part of the board or a worksheet. You can then add to this list, based on ideas and suggestions from the class.

Procedure

1 Tell your learners the two stories below, or two of your own stories of the same length.

Story 1 I was driving home with a friend. It was evening. As we turned a corner, I was sure I saw a huge black cat, the size of a tiger, crossing the road. I screamed. My friend didn't see anything. She said it was just the shadow of the car in the lamplight.

Story 2 I was putting up shelves in a friend's house. I heard a knocking on the other side of the wall. It was a regular knock, as if someone on the other side was putting shelves up too. I began knocking a little faster, then a little slower. The person on the other side answered me, first slow, then fast. After a bit, I became curious.

I walked round the house to have a look. There was nothing there, no trees, no people, and it was an outside wall, so there were no neighbours. I was so shocked that I stood outside the front door. I didn't want to go in again.

2 Ask the learners to suggest a 'label' for each story, explaining the 'type'.
   - a soap opera
   - a ghost story
   - a mystery story
   - a thriller
   - a detective story
   - a travel story
   - a science-fiction story
   - a space story
   - a romance.

Ask how they know.

3 Write on the board their suggestions for each story. Ask them to justify their choices. Here are some suggestions made by teachers from Sweden and Switzerland.

	Story 1	Story 2
Story type:	a mystery story	a ghost story
	a detective story	a parallel-universe story
	a science-fiction story	a science-fiction story

4 Now divide the class into groups of three or four, and ask each group to choose one of the stories. In their group, they must also decide what *type* their story belongs to.

5 When they have decided, ask each group to write a short explanation of the story so far, based on the type of story they have chosen. Their explanation should be very brief, just one or two phrases or sentences.

Example **Story 1**

A mystery story:	is the cat real or not? Is the driver of the car mad or not?
A detective story:	mysterious crimes happen at night. Poncinello the detective suspects a giant cat.
A science-fiction story:	the cat is an alien from outer space, visible only to the chosen few.

Story 2

A ghost story:	the tapping is the ghost of a person who lived in the house next door before it fell down.
A parallel-universe story:	the wall is the entrance to another universe, and the builder is being invited in.
A science-fiction story:	a scientist can build houses that take on the habits and characteristics of their owners.

6 Now explain that each group is going to write the 'blurb' for the back of the book. The 'blurb' needs to:

- explain very briefly what the story is about, without giving away the ending
- make it clear what TYPE of story this is
- give readers a reason for buying the book.

Example Here are some key phrases that might help. You can write them on the board as a guide.

- *This _____ (adjective) books tells the story of_____
  _____ .*
- *It is a wonderful _____ (story type) that every reader will find
  _____ (adjective).*

With a less advanced class, it may be useful to brainstorm adjectives and phrases that are relevant to each story type. Encourage your learners to use dictionaries.

- science fiction: strange, extraordinary
- thriller: spine-chilling, terrifying, full of suspense
- detective story: exciting, keeps you guessing.

7   When groups have finished their 'blurbs', ask them to choose a title for their story and write this clearly at the top of the page.

8   Display the 'blurbs' around the room, or ask groups to read them aloud. Ask each member of the class to choose just one story they would like to buy. At the end of the lesson, have a vote on their favourite story.

Variation

With pre-intermediate learners, it may be possible to conduct the discussion (steps 1–6) in the mother tongue, and ask them to write the story title at step 7 in English.

Follow-up

Check whether the learners have chosen adjectives that are appropriate to their story type.

Encourage them to use dictionaries to check this for themselves. A common error is to find the 'perfect' adjective and use it too many times. Ask groups to edit their 'blurbs' to make sure they use each adjective only once.

A more advanced class could now use the 'blurb' as the basis for continuing the story. Ask the class to finish their story and bring their final version to the next class. The editing checklists in Chapter 10 could then be used for peer correction.

Learners could also be encouraged to use their 'blurbs' as the starting point for improvisation. Chapter 9 will give you ideas for turning classroom writing tasks into short sketches, role-plays and group storytelling.

1.3 Story connections: the dancer and the clown

Level Intermediate and above

Time 30 minutes

Aims To look at cohesion in sentences; to look at how cohesive markers (conjunctions) can change the meaning of sentences.

Procedure

1   Write the sentences below on the board.

A The dancer died, **then** the clown lost his job.
B The dancer died **because** the clown lost his job.

Ask your class to discuss them. The following questions may be used as a guide:
• What is the difference between the two sentences?
• What do you know about the people in sentence A?
• What do you know about the people in sentence B?
• Who is broken-hearted in each sentence?

2 Divide your class into two groups:

Group A should write a short explanation of sentence A.
Group B should write a short explanation of sentence B.

Example Pepin loved Graciella, but she never looked at him. One day, she left to become a dancer in the circus. He followed her there. He could not dance, so he learnt to be a clown. Every day he laughed and laughed, but really he was crying. Then, one day, she fell from the high trapeze and died. The clown could not laugh now. He lost his job because he could no longer be a clown.

3 Now, write the table below on the board and ask the learners to choose their own words from columns 1, 2, 3, 4, 5, and 6.

	1	2	3	4	5	6
The	dancer	died	then	the	clown	died of grief.
	singer	disappeared	because		professor	lost his job.
	farmer		so		astronaut	
	librarian		while		shopkeeper	
	pilot		when		bus-driver	
	soldier		after		fruit-seller	

Example The pilot disappeared, so the astronaut died of grief.
The librarian died when the shopkeeper ran away.

4 In pairs, ask them to explain their sentence and 'tell the story'.

Variation

At step 2, read your learners the story about Pepin and Graciella. Ask them to tell you if this story describes sentence A or sentence B, and to give you their reasons.

1.4 Starting at the end: the Great Wall walk

Level Pre-intermediate and above
Time 30 minutes
Aims To look at how the opening sentence in a text changes text organization; to look at verb forms and time sequences.

Procedure

1 Tell, read, or show your learners the story on the next page. You could also choose one of the other stories in this book, or adapt the story to match the level of your class.

2 Now divide your class into two groups.

Group 1 are going to retell the story, starting in the *middle*, at sentence 1.

Group 2 are going to retell the story, starting at the *end*, at sentence 2.

Worksheet 1.4

Meilin and Chenpei agreed to make a special test of their love.

They agreed to walk the Great Wall of China: one would start at one end, and the other would start at the other end. They would walk, and walk, until they met in the middle.

They prepared for their special journey by making themselves strong and fit. The day the cherry tree blossomed, they started their journey.

They travelled many miles in opposite directions to find the beginning of the wall. And then they both started the walk. Meilin travelled east. Chenpei travelled west.

1 Meilin walked for days, and weeks, and months. She became strong, and brave, and burnt by the sun, and tired, and fit. But still she did not meet her love. And one day, she saw to her surprise, the other end of the wall.

2 She had walked the whole journey, but, along the whole wall, Chenpei was nowhere to be seen.

Photocopiable © Oxford University Press

Ask each group to work together and decide how the story will need to be changed.

3 When the stories are finished, ask each person from group 1 to find a partner in group 2. Ask them to compare their stories. The following questions may be used as a guide.
  • In what order are the events described in each story?
  • What are the tenses used?
  • Which version do you prefer?

4 You might also ask the learners to consider the following changes in verb forms:

Their versions may involve the continuous/progressive aspect: *She had been walking for days and weeks and months. She had been growing fit and strong.*

They may need to use 'flashbacks'—looking back at events that are already completed. This will require the past perfect tense: *She had started her journey the day of the first cherry blossom.*

5 Ask the partners now to work out why Chenpei never appeared. What happened to him?

Example Meilin and Chenpei passed each other in the night. They did not see each other.

Now he is at the other end of the wall, and he too is heartbroken.

Follow-up

For homework, the learners could tell their story of why Chenpei never appeared and what happened to him.

This activity can be tried out with any story the learners have written or read. Ask them to return to a story they have prepared in other activities in this book, and tell the same story, but using the last sentence at the beginning.

1.5 Changing endings: changing places

Even real-life events may have more than one ending. For one person, a story that ends with a long sea journey is a happy ending full of exciting possibilities; for another, that same ending may be tragic, full of loss for what is left behind and fear of the future. This activity explores the fact that stories can have different endings for each of the characters involved.

Level Pre-intermediate and above

Time 30 minutes

Aims To look at different ways of ending a text; to develop a text from closing lines; to predict text content from closing lines.

Procedure

1 Tell your learners this story. You can change the story so the actions are typical ones for the learners in your class. Ideally, you should memorize the story so you can 'tell' it without a text. Chapter 9 will help you to do this.

2 Now, ask your learners to suggest what happens next. Elicit possibilities and write them on the board.

Worksheet 1.5

After a few years of living happily together, a husband one day said to his wife,

'It's all right for you. I do all the work. I leave early in the morning, drive through the traffic, spend all day in the office, sit in meetings for hours on end, have to be polite to foolish and stupid people. All you do is sit by the fire, sing to the baby, and make soup. It's not fair.'

'OK,' said the wife, who herself had been a company manager before she had the baby, 'let's change places for a day. You stay at home and sing to the baby, and I'll go to the office and sit in meetings.'

Examples The man has a terrible day and realizes how clever his wife is.
The man has a wonderful day and decides to give up his job.
The wife has a wonderful day and is offered a job in the company.
The wife has a terrible day and realizes how clever her husband is.
The wife has a terrible day and realizes her husband must be very unhappy doing this job.

3 Ask the learners to choose the story ending they like best and to write it down on a piece of paper.

Take in the pieces of paper, and shuffle them. Ask your class to work in groups of two or three, and give each group one piece of paper. Tell them to use the story ending to:

- plan the story orally
- make notes while they plan
- use the notes to write a version for homework.

Variation

Learners could also develop their own 'exchange' stories: parent and child, teacher and student, people from different countries, or people in different jobs, exchange places for the day.

Follow-up

Ask the learners to exchange stories orally or in written form with another group.

Ask them to:

- read the final lines of their story first
- predict the middle of the story, on the basis of the final lines
- compare their prediction with the version already prepared.

1.6 Split-second stories: Tomaso's magic hut

Stories can take place in a split second or across a thousand years.

Level Intermediate and above

Time 20 minutes

Aims To match events to a timescale; to use appropriate words to describe time (nouns, adverbs, verb tenses).

Procedure

1 Write the words below on the board:
  a second
  two minutes
  an hour
  a day
  a year
  a decade
  a century
  a millennium.

Learners could also suggest further timescales. For example: a week, a fortnight, or a month.

2 Ask the learners: *What events could you describe in each of these timescales?* Ask the learners to make suggestions. You could use some of those in the box below as a starting point.

a second	the moment a bomb drops the moment of drowning the moment a baby is born love at first sight
two minutes	the time a tree takes to fall down the time between thunder and a huge crack of lightning the time between a deep breath and a huge snore falling asleep
an hour	a bus journey a train journey
a day	a walk around a city a day in the life of someone
a year	the first year in a new school meeting, falling in love and getting married getting pregnant and having a baby leaving a job, looking for a new one, finding it, starting the new job the first year at university the first year emigrating to another country
a decade	growing from child to adult a village turning into a town an adult going from rags to riches
a century	three generations in a family a village turning into a town then into a big city

3 Ask the learners to choose among these situations and timescales one that interests them. They should now tell their story, in answer to the questions:

Who is your character?
Where does your story take place?
What happens in the story?

Examples

4 When they have planned their story, ask them to retell it to a partner for him or her to guess the timescale of the story: a second, a minute, an hour, or a century?

5 After ten minutes, ask the learners to give you a show of hands to determine:

- How many listeners guessed correctly?
- How many split-second stories were there?
- How many one-year stories were there?

Worksheet 1.6
Split-second story

Jay was swimming in the sea, when a huge wave came. Then it went quiet and suddenly he saw his dead grandmother sitting quietly, and his first schoolteacher. 'How did you get here?!' he started to shout, but his mouth filled with water. Then he saw his mother. 'Do look after yourself,' she said. He started to run after her, but his legs kept floating in the air. Then, he saw three monkeys jump out of a tree. One tried to steal his hat. He reached out to hold on to his hat, but it wasn't there. 'Oh well, I'll just relax,' he thought. Suddenly, there was a huge bang. Everything went bright and dazzling. Then, a hundred miles away, he heard: 'Just in time. He nearly drowned but I think we've saved him!'

Century story

Tomaso lived in a hut in the middle of a field. He was very happy there, until one day he ate a magic carrot and fell asleep. No one could wake him up. He slept, and slept, and slept. A month, a year, ten years, fifty years went by. His children grew up, became old and died. His grandchildren grew up, became old and died. Then one day, he woke up. His hut was just the same as the day he fell asleep. He walked out of the hut, and he couldn't understand what he saw. The sky was filled with tall buildings and grey smoke, the field was covered with concrete, and strange zooming metal things screamed up and down, with lights flashing, and people shouting. Tomaso looked around. Then he said, 'I think I'll go to sleep again,' and went back inside his hut.

Collect the stories in a class storybook, ordered according to timescale, from seconds to millennium. The book could then be used as a reading resource for other classes, who could continue to add to it.

2
Sources of stories

There was once a belief that imaginative ideas came from nowhere (*ex nihilo*), and leapt into the mind of the storyteller as if by magic. But if this were true, not only would many of our best stories never have been told, they would not have been nearly as interesting. The best storytellers, including Shakespeare himself, borrowed stories from history, popular myth, rumours, and gossip. Our own memories, lives, dreams, and friendships are a rich story resource, but so is the world around us, with pictures, songs, newspaper headlines, television programmes, and conversations overheard. We do not have to wait for a divine spark to leap into our minds; in fact, it is far better that we do not, but rather look around us and find the stories that are already in front of our eyes. This chapter helps us to do so by encouraging us to look at other stories, opening lines, the stories in familiar streets and buildings, in our own family, and in our everyday lives, and to think about how these can 'grow' into new stories of our own.

2.1 Start with an opening line: Candy the giant mango

Level Intermediate and above

Time 30 minutes

Aims To look at the opening lines of stories as starting points; to use variations of simple statement sentences as starting points for stories; to fill subject and complement slots in a sentence.

Procedure

1 Choose one of the lines below that matches your learners' level, and write it on the board. You may need to explain the words in *italics*, depending on your learners' level.

Example All happy families *resemble* (are similar to) one another, but each unhappy family is unhappy in its own way. (Tolstoy)

The past is a foreign country. They do things differently there. (Hartley, L. P., *The Go-between*)

When Gregor Samsa awoke one morning from *uneasy* (disturbing) dreams, he found himself *transformed* (changed) in his bed into a gigantic insect. (Kafka, Franz, *Metamorphosis*)

Nothing is more *deadly* (dangerous) than a *deserted* (empty) waiting street. (Harper Lee)

2 Ask your learners to choose the word they think is the most interesting or surprising in the sentence. Ask them to share their choice with a partner. Then ask them to tell the class their ideas, and underline each of the chosen words.

Example When <u>Gregor Samsa</u> awoke one morning from uneasy dreams, he found himself transformed in his bed into a <u>gigantic</u> insect.

3 Now delete each of the underlined words, and asked the class to fill in a word of their own choice. They can do this orally or make a note of the changed word on a piece of paper.

Example When Candy, the sweetshop girl, awoke one morning from uneasy dreams, she found herself transformed in her bed into a giant mango.

4 Now ask them to share their revised sentences in groups of two or three. Ask them to choose the best sentence and then develop the story by asking questions.

Examples
- *What did he/she feel?*
- *What did he/she do next?*
- *Who did he/she meet on the way?*
- *What did they think/say/do?*
- *How long did he/she remain this way?*

5 When the groups have developed the story orally, they can work with a designated scribe to write down their versions.

6 Ask groups to exchange their written stories and edit for:
- any other ideas that it would be interesting to develop
- any other information they would like about the characters or events
- any changes to the language to make it clearer, more interesting, or more accurate.

Variation 1

This activity can also be combined with 3.1 'Naming people', in order to fill in the name at the beginning of the sentence.

Variation 2

A more advanced group might like to:
- bring in story openings of their own that they have enjoyed
- combine a number of story openings into one.
  For example, 'Nothing is more deadly than an unhappy family'.

Comment

You may want to start to build up a 'bank' of interesting story openings that you either find yourself, or which are suggested by your learners.

2.2 Start with newspaper headlines: joining up the lines

Level Elementary and above

Time 40 minutes

Aims To identify theme and meaning in newspaper headlines; to find thematic connections between texts; to use the simple past for news stories.

Preparation

During the lesson before this activity, ask your learners to go to the newsagent and read and note down five headlines related to the same topic in different English papers. If your learners are at pre-intermediate level, you could ask them to read the front pages of newspapers in their mother tongue, or those they have at home, and note down five headlines. You could also use simplified English headlines at stage 1, tailoring them so they are explicit to your learners. The aim is not to generate ambiguity, but to activate interest.

The reason for suggesting that you use three to five headlines at stage 1 is that writers sometimes respond not to a single newspaper article, but to clusters of articles or headlines that raise a specific theme, concern, or memory.

Procedure

1 Write a cluster of three to five headlines on the board. Next to each of the following examples, you will find a possible explanation for the headline. Ask your learners to give other possible explanations.

Examples a *Leak reveals fear over release of dangerous criminals* = News that dangerous criminals may leave prison.

b *How did the men of Harby cope when their women left?* = Women leave their men behind for a week as part of a television programme. What did the men do?

c *The video game with an offer you can't refuse* = Violent video games for sale.

d *I think I'll speak today, says mute piano man* = Mysterious man found in wet clothes, cannot speak, but can play the piano beautifully. No one knows who he is.

2 Divide the class in groups of three and start a group discussion along the following lines.

Choose two of the headlines that you think have some connection.

- What is the connection?
- What do you feel about this? Do you think this news is: good, bad, worrying, interesting?
- Make a statement about the news.
- Now write a third newspaper headline that gives you the same 'feeling'.

Here are some learners' responses to the headlines above.

Example I choose:

a and **c**, because both are about violence in our society.

b and **c**, because this is what television does. We do all things for television.

a and **b**, because men become criminal without women.

These are the headlines written by this group of learners. Any of the headlines could be the starting point for a story.

- Numbers of bad crimes in small town get bigger
- Whole town becomes mad because of TV programme!
- All children run away together from high crime place

3 Ask the learners to develop their own story headline, using the simple past for narratives. They can answer questions to help them.

- What happened next?
- Why did it happen?
- Who are the main characters in the stories?

Comment

You may want to start building up a bank of interesting newspaper headlines that you find yourself, or which are suggested by your learners.

2.3 Start with a proverb or saying: free birds and captive kings

Level Elementary and above

Time 30 minutes

Aim To look at the language and meaning of idioms and proverbs.

Procedure

1 Choose some of the proverbs below that you think your learners will understand and enjoy, and write them on the board. You could also choose proverbs that are familiar to your learners. If your learners are at an elementary level, you may choose to do stages 1–3 in their mother tongue.

Examples When elephants battle, the ants perish. (Cambodian)
If you chase two hares, you will not catch either. (Russian)
Talk does not cook rice. (Chinese)
After the rain, there is no need for an umbrella. (Bulgarian)

Little brooks make great rivers. (French)
Better to be a free bird than a captive king. (Danish)
The heaviest burden is an empty pocket. (Yiddish)
It takes a village to raise a child. (African)
It is one thing to cackle and another to lay an egg. (Ecuadorean)
Step by step, one ascends the staircase. (Turkish)
Little by little, the cotton thread becomes a loincloth. (Africa-
   Dahomey)
Anger is a bad adviser. (Hungary)
Eggs must not quarrel with stones. (Jamaican)
Eyes can see everything except themselves. (Serbo-Croatian)
Haste makes waste. (English)
Every hill has its valley. (Italian)

2   Ask your learners to work with a partner, and plan a short
    explanation of each proverb. After five minutes, ask partners to share
    their explanations with the class.

Examples   *Better to be a free bird than a captive king.*
    Explanation: to be free is the most important thing. Money and
    power are useless if you are not free.

    It takes a village to raise a child.
    Explanation: it is not only parents who help a child grow up. It is all
    the people around, the way people live, and if they are good, honest,
    and loving people.

3   Ask the learners to choose the one proverb that interests them most.
    Ask them to plan with their partner. Give them some ideas. They
    could write notes in order to give an oral account of their story.
    How did this proverb come to be?
    What was the original story behind the proverb?

4   After ten minutes, ask each pair to tell their story to the rest of the
    class. Tell other learners to listen carefully, and decide which proverb
    is being described.

    With elementary learners, this stage could be in English or in their
    mother tongue. If you can, act as a 'translator', so the story is shared
    both in the mother tongue and in English.

Follow-up

Make a note of interesting proverbs or idioms or ask the learners to
tell you proverbs or idioms from their own cultures and mother
tongues. If they can, they could also explain the meaning of the
proverb, and the story behind them.

2.4 Start with a writer's notebook: bus-queue stories

Level Elementary and above

Time This activity should proceed in three stages:

STAGE 1: setting homework, 10 minutes

STAGE 2: the learners will need to keep a notebook for five minutes a day for one week

STAGE 3: classroom follow-up, 30 minutes

Aims To use fleeting images and experiences as a starting point for a story; to encourage learners to start a notebook of ideas and observations; to practise the connection between fragments.

Procedure

1 At the end of one of your lessons, spend ten minutes introducing learners to the idea of the notebook. Ask them to discuss these questions with a partner:

- Do any of you keep a journal or a diary?
- If so, what do you record/write in it?
- Have any of you read the diary or journal of another person?
- If so, what did you find interesting?

2 After five minutes, ask learners to share their observations. List their ideas on the board.

Examples What I write in my diary.
What I enjoy about diaries I have read.

feelings
conversations
scenes
description of places
events.

3 Explain to the learners that you are going to ask them to start a writer's notebook, in which they may note down just one small idea each day. Each entry need be only a phrase, a few words, or a single sentence, but they will capture one small thing remembered or experienced each day. Explain that the main idea behind their keeping a notebook can be to record small things which apparently have no significance, such as something new they ate that day, seeing an interesting face in the bus queue, or buying a new pair of shoes.

You could prepare a reference sheet for them such as the one below:

> **Worksheet 2.4**
> ## Starting a writer's notebook
>
> Record in your notebook just *one thing* that you notice each day. It could be something you hear, or see, or do. It could be: a sound, a person, an object, or a conversation you hear.
>
> It can be very short: just two words, or just a picture.
>
> You may write it in your own language.
>
> You may just write key words.
>
> Write the date by each record.
>
> Spend five minutes each day writing down your ideas.

4 Ask the learners to write one entry each day for a week, and to bring their notes to the lesson in one week's time.

5 In the lesson, ask them to work in groups of four, sharing phrases, words, or ideas from their notebooks.

6 After five minutes, explain that each group is going to make a short record of their observations for the week. Draw up the chart below on the board. Ask the learners to suggest other categories, and to suggest examples for each one. When the idea of the chart is clear, ask them to return to their groups and complete the chart with their own observations.

Objects	Expressions/gestures
photo of grandparents' wedding a bus ticket	a baby smiling a girl waving goodbye a boy about to serve in tennis
Places	**People**
a bus queue a station platform full of people	a boy begging under a railway bridge, sitting on a blanket

7 After ten minutes, check the progress of the group records. Explain that these observations and ideas are to form part of a story. They can choose the ideas, scenes, people, and objects that interest them most. They can choose ideas taken from another member of the group. They can group and organize them in any way they wish. The aim is to connect their favourite ideas to make a story. The story could be a real-life one describing their actual experience during the week, or an invented one.

8   To help your learners structure their story, suggest they:

- write an opening sentence to set the scene.
- introduce a problem.
- introduce a conversation.

The story does not need to be complete. It can end with a question, or an unsolved problem, like the story below:

> She met him waiting for a bus. When the bus arrived, the driver said, 'Where's your ticket?'
>
> 'I don't have one,' she said. 'But please, let me on. I'm in such a hurry and my journey is very important.'
>
> 'Here, take my ticket!' the young man behind her said. 'Please, I really do insist.'
>
> She climbed on the bus. As it drove away down the street, she waved goodbye to him through the window.
>
> 'How kind he is! Will I ever see him again to say thank you properly?'

Variation 1

You could also ask the learners to collect 'objects' as a record of each day of the week, instead of writing notes. You could make 'rules' for these objects:

- they must be small enough to fit into your pocket (for example, a photo, a spoon, a small toy, or a drawing)
- they must belong to you or belong to nobody (for example, a leaf or a stone).

The story activity could then be built around these objects.

Variation 2

Ask your learners, at the end of each day, to spend five minutes making a drawing of one event or image from the day.

Collect these as 'ingredients for stories' and start the activity at stage 7 above.

Comment

If your learners develop the 'habit' of keeping a writer's notebook, sharing observations from it could be used as a classroom filler and lead to a story whenever needed.

2.5 Start with another story

The best writers have borrowed stories from others. But a borrowed story is just the starting point. You can make a story your own by using the ideas in this activity.

Level Elementary and above

Time 30 minutes

Aim To look at the parts of a story that can be changed; to look at lexical items in a story, and the ways they can be changed; to look at the effect of vocabulary changes on overall meaning.

Procedure

1   Ask your class to think about a 'good story' they have heard, seen, or read recently. It could be:

  • a film or television play they have seen
  • a real-life story recounted by a friend
  • a story read in a comic, newspaper, or magazine
  • a story read in a novel
  • a story read to them or remembered from childhood.

2   Ask your class to work in groups of two or three, and tell the 'good story' briefly.

  If your learners are at elementary level, they can do this stage in their mother tongue. Ask the group to choose the story they liked best.

3   Now ask them to work with the story they have chosen. Copy the chart below on the board, or make copies so learners can work with it.

  Change the characters:
  Change the boys to girls.
  Change the girls to boys.
  Give new names to the characters.

  Change the place where the story happens.

  Change the ending:
  Make a happy ending sad.
  Make a sad ending happy.

4   Ask the class to discuss any other changes they could make to the story. Write their ideas on the board.

  Make an old person young.
  Make a young person old.
  Make the bad person good.
  Make the good person bad.
  Make a serious person silly or funny.
  Introduce an animal.
  Make the story happen today/long ago.
  Make the story happen in this town/city/village/school/college.

5 Ask the groups to work with these ideas for ten minutes. Tell them to write notes with their ideas. Remind them they should have:

- a name/description of main characters
- a place where the story happens
- a follow-up for the situation.

6 Now ask your learners to prepare the story to tell the class orally, using all their voices as characters and narrators, and to connect all their ideas into a short written summary of their story.

Variation

You could use a story in this book, or a story of your own, instead of stages 1–2. The index lists all the stories in this book. Activity 6.7 gives an example of story retelling, using a sentence completion technique.

Follow-up

Build up a bank of short summaries of folk tales and nursery tales that could be 'transformed' in the same way. Keep them in a file in your classroom, so you can use them as 'fillers' in other classes.

2.6 Start with a picture: city monkeys

Many very popular stories written recently are about pictures or paintings. For example, *The Girl with the Pearl Earring* (Tracey Chevalier) is about a painting by Vermeer, *Headlong* (Michael Frayn) is about a painting by Breughel, and *The Da Vinci Code* (Dan Brown) is about a painting by Leonardo da Vinci.
Writers can:

- tell a story about how or why the picture was painted
- tell the story of the people or scene in the painting
- tell the story of the painter or photographer.

Level Elementary and above

Time 30 minutes

Aim To look at pictures as source for a story; to find connections between pictures; to look at sequencing and coherence between ideas.

Procedure

The following are three variations on the same picture activity. You can choose the one most suited to your learners' level and interests.

Picture activity 1

1 Divide the learners into groups of three or four. Ask each student to draw any image or picture they like on a blank sheet of paper. Explain they do not need to be great artists! Simple line drawings are fine. Ask them to do this individually and not look at one another's drawings.

2   When the pictures are completed, ask the learners to share them with others in the group.

Their task is now to invent a story that includes all three of their pictures.

3   After ten minutes, ask each group to tell their story to others in the class.

4   As a further development of this activity, the learners could put their pictures at the front of the class in a random sequence. As they tell the story, the learners could suggest what the correct sequence of pictures should be.

Picture activity 2
Materials

Cut out and collect pictures from magazines. You should have enough pictures for each group of learners to have three.

Procedure

1   Divide the learners in groups of three or four.
2   Hand out to each group a set of three pictures from your collection.
3   Ask each group to organize the three pictures into any sequence they like, and invent a story that connects them all.
4   When they have completed their story, ask them to join another group. They should shuffle the pictures to change the sequence, and retell their story. The members of the other group should listen, and rearrange the pictures in the correct sequence.

Picture activity 3: Story captions
Materials

For this activity, you will need a cartoon strip from a newspaper or from a magazine. Blank out the captions from the cartoon strip. Alternatively, you could use the cartoon strip below.

Procedure

1   Give each group of learners three or four pictures from a cartoon strip, with the captions blanked out.
2   Now ask the learners to write the captions in. They should fill in:

- thought bubbles
- caption underneath the picture.

3   Give the learners ten minutes to finish their task. Collect and display all the cartoons round the room. Ask the learners to circulate, reading one another's ideas.

Photocopiable © Oxford University Press

Variation 1

Divide the class into groups of three to four and give one picture to each group.

Ask the learners to imagine there is something just outside the picture that they cannot see. Ask them what they think is going to happen next and to tell the story.

Example   A huge spaceship in the sky
A huge crack of lightning about to strike

Variation 2

Divide the class into groups of three to four and give one picture to each group. Ask them to imagine something unusual dropped into the picture. Why is it there? How did it get there? Ask them to tell the story.

Variation 3

Divide the class into groups of three to four and give one picture to each group. Ask them to imagine thought bubbles coming out of the people in the picture. What are they thinking?

Variation 4

Divide the class into groups of three to four and give one picture to each group. Ask them to imagine speech bubbles coming out of the people in the picture. What are they saying?

Variation 5

Divide the class into groups of three to four and give one picture to each group. Ask them to imagine the picture is being used as evidence in a crime investigation. What is the crime? What is the evidence in the picture? Ask them to tell the story.

Follow-up 1

Learners could exchange cartoons and edit one another's texts, using the editing checklists in Chapter 10.

Follow-up 2

You could also build up a 'bank' of pictures. These could be: photos, postcards, birthday cards, magazine pictures, newspaper pictures, or drawings. Ask the learners to add to this collection, and keep it in the classroom for regular use.

Acknowledgements

Picture activity 1 was invented by Bao Dat, who demonstrated it to us with great success at MICELT, Melaka, in April 2005.

2.7 Start with family stories

Level Elementary and above

Time This activity should proceed in three stages:

STAGE 1: setting homework, 10 minutes

STAGE 2: learners will need to have a conversation with one of their family members at home

STAGE 3: homework follow-up, 30 minutes

Aims To summarize a story; to use reported speech; to formulate open questions.

Procedure

1 Tell the learners that for homework they are going to interview a member of their family, if that is possible. If not, they should interview a friend or neighbour. The interview can be either in the shared mother tongue or in English. The learners' task is to ask this person to tell them:

- a memory of being a child, or
- a memory of life in another country, or
- a memory of growing up.

Elicit from your class some of the interview questions that might be helpful. Point out the difference between open questions, which elicit long and reflective answers, and closed questions, which elicit short, yes/no answers. Ask them to translate this same difference into questions in their mother tongue. Make sure each student has at least two open-ended questions they are happy with.

2 Set a date about one week in advance for the learners to bring the results of their interviews. Ask them to record the interview in the way that suits them best.

Examples Make notes during the interview, using just key words and phrases, so they can reconstruct the interview later.

Record the interview on tape, by agreement with the interviewee, if it is practical for them to do so.

Make a written record of the interview as soon as it is over, and while the answers are fresh in their mind. Then check with the interviewee that the record is correct.

Open questions:

Tell me about some happy moments you had as a child
Tell me about some of your best friends as a child
Tell me about the games you used to play as a child
What was it like at school?
What did you do in the school holidays?

Topics to talk about

Tell me about…
food
pets
holidays
games
relatives
groups, clubs, or societies
what lessons/the teachers were like at school
when you were a child

Photocopiable © Oxford University Press

3 After one week, ask the learners to bring their notes back to class. They should work in a group of three or four, retelling the interview in their own words using: 'He said/she said that …', 'I asked him/her if/whether …'

4 When the groups have shared their interview accounts, ask them to choose any interview they have heard which interests them, and to rewrite it as a story and to give the speakers new names.

Variation

The interviews can be written up in several ways. Select the format that suits the level of your class best—dialogue is the easiest and reported conversation the most difficult.

- as a dialogue, using first person throughout and reconstructing the conversation
- as a story, in which the interviewee becomes he/she, and the memories are recounted as actual events
- as a reported conversation, like a newspaper article, in which reported speech is used.

2.8 Start with local stories: the king's dinner

Very often there are stories about a local area, or about people who lived there, which are partly fact and partly legend. This activity invites learners to share with others a little bit of this 'local history', and turn it into story. If they are living away from home, it can also be an opportunity to inform others about their own region. Eventually, you may decide to share the stories with learners in another area or country, for example by linking up with another school and exchanging stories through the internet.

Level **Intermediate and above**

Time **30 minutes**

Aims **To look at how real places, fact, and fiction can be combined to make a story; to turn information into narrative.**

Procedure

1 Tell the learners they are going to tell a story about where they live. Ask them the questions below and give them a minute between each to think. Ask them to note down key words for each question.

Do you know a real story/legend about this?

your home/house: Who lived in your home before you? Why did they leave?

your city: How did your city or town get its name?

a building in the city: Is there a story about a building in your town/suburb/street/village? For example, why was it built? Who lived in it? Has a ghost ever been seen inside it? If not, invent one!

visitors to your city: Has your town/street/village ever had any strange, famous or historical visitors?

features of the landscape: Where do the names of the rocks, river, mountain shapes in your region come from?

If not, could you invent a story?

---

2 When you have finished, ask the learners to compare their notes with a partner. If you have learners from the same region, they could work together to explore local stories.

3 Ask the learners to plan a story about their local area: fact or fiction, myth, or modern legend. They could start their story with the questions:

- Who is in the story?
- Where are they?
- What happens in the story?
- Which particular building/street/city/feature of the landscape is important in the story?

4 After 20 minutes, ask the learners to retell their stories in groups. While they listen, they should guess: *Is this a true story? Is this a local legend? Or has my classmate just invented it?*

Worksheet 2.8 is a true story/local legend about my own town, Totnes, in South Devon. The king in the story is Charles I and it took place just before the Civil War, which ended in his execution.

Worksheet 2.8
The king's dinner party

Four hundred years ago, the king came to visit my town. He brought with him all his servants, his cook, his dressmaker, and his favourite army of fifty men. They each brought two horses and a pile of dirty clothes from the long journey. The king and all these men moved into the town hall, and ordered the best meat, vegetables, cheeses, and wine, breads, and biscuits. The washerwomen burnt their hands washing the clothes. Farmers slaughtered their best cows and chickens, all the apple trees were stripped of apples, the cheese and wine stores of the town were emptied, and the bakers worked all night, stoking their ovens. The king and his men drank and ate, and ate and drank, until there was nothing left. Then they got up, and left all the washing-up for the local people without paying the bill.

Later, the country decided it was time to get rid of the king and have a republic. Everyone in England had to choose between the king and the people. For the people of Totnes it was easy: they certainly never wanted a king to come for dinner again.

Follow-up

Learners could write their stories for homework. They could then edit their own or a fellow student's story, using one or more of the editing checklists in Chapter 10.

3
Story stars

The most important part of every story is the people in it. Whether these are people we like and admire, or fear and despise, it is important that they are people who interest us. A good story will invite us into the world of the main character, and make us care about what happens to him/her. For many storytellers and readers, character is the very heart of good story. In this chapter, we will look at how we can 'find' characters and develop them. We will look at characters talking, thinking, searching, choosing, losing, and winning. We will also look at how we can describe characters so they come alive, and drop them into situations where they start to change and grow.

The activities in this chapter can all be used with the editing checklist for characterization in Chapter 10.

3.1 Naming people: moaning Mona Lisa

Level Elementary and above

Time 10 minutes

Aims To understand and analyse names; to look at word association and connotation.

Procedure

1 Write the following examples of nicknames on the board. When you have done this activity once with your class, you can use nicknames your learners have suggested.

Mungo	Biribi	Shereritu	Chelaka	Candy
Zsomle	Mamouch	Susu	Fujo	Don Foglio
Patipuse	Mingo	Wawa	Nangi	Mona Lisa

2 Tell your class these are all real nicknames suggested by learners and teachers. Ask them to guess:
- *Which of them are pets?*
- *Which of them are adults?*
- *Which of them are children?*
- *What might the pets/people look like?*

3   Elicit the ideas of the class. Make it clear there are no 'right' answers, but that all their suggestions are interesting and useful, and show the power of 'names'.

4   Now explain to them that the following are real-life explanations or meanings for some of the names. Can they match similar definitions to the rest of the names in the box above?

Patipuse: little thumb, from the French for ' little thumb': *petit pouce*, to describe a new-born baby with no hair.

Zsomle: Hungarian word for 'bread roll', to describe a honey-coloured dog the colour of a freshly baked bread roll

Wawa: nickname for a small child who pronounced the word 'water' as 'wawa'

Mona Lisa: nickname for a great-aunt who moaned a lot: 'moaner Lisa'.

5   Ask your learners to share their explanations or meanings for the rest of the names with the class. You can discuss with them how they made their choices. In Variations, there is a list of possible reasons. You can also make it clear that there are no 'right' answers.

Examples   Shereritu, the bad-tempered teacher: because 'shereritu' sounds like someone shouting and scolding.

Candy, the sweetshop girl: because she works at the sweetshop and/or she wears green and white striped clothes like a peppermint.

6   Now ask each learner to choose *one* name that interests them, and write a short description/explanation of their own. They should write each name and definition on a label for future story activities.

Variation 1

You could also use photographs of people as a starting point for this activity, and ask:

What name would you give each person in the photograph? Why?

Variation 2

A more advanced class might want to discuss how they arrived at their interpretations of the names.

Was it:

- an association with other words?
- cultural knowledge or information?
- knowledge of the world?
- personal experiences?
- a reminder of other characters in stories or real life?
- the sound of the word?

Variation 3

In a culture or class where nicknames are often used, you could also ask learners to write down a nickname they remember from childhood or use today, for example, that of a pet, a best friend, a teacher, or a relation. Then work through the procedures from step 1 onwards, using the learners' own examples.

Acknowledgements

Nicknames in this activity derive from students and teachers at Janus Pannonius University, Pecs, Hungary; Irish Teachers' Association, Dublin, Ireland; students in Hungary, Poland, Plymouth, and Oxford.

3.2 Story stars: people in stories, people in life

This activity invites learners to think about people in their own lives as starting points for stories.

Level Elementary and above

Time 10–40 minutes

Aims To work with vocabulary to describe people, jobs, descriptive labels, and nicknames; to use short phrases *someone who...*, *someone with...*; to use the adverbs *always, never*; to encourage learners to develop characters by looking at their typical features and small changes.

Materials

A set of four blank labels for each learner.

Preparation

Bring to the class a set of blank labels for the learners to use in their writing activity. Alternatively, learners could make their own blank labels at step 5 below, by tearing a blank sheet of paper into four.

Procedure

1 Draw on the board a series of three circles. Ask the learners to write their names at the centre of the circle.

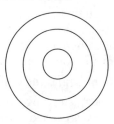

2 Now explain that they are going to write the names of friends, family, pets and teachers in the other circles. The people they are closest to should go in the circles that are closer to their names, the people who are less close should go in the outer circles.

3 After ten minutes, ask the learners to work with a partner and explain the choices they have made for each circle.

4 Now tell your class to choose FOUR of the characters in their circles. Ask them to write a short phrase for each character, using the ideas below.

A _____1_____ in _____2_____.

A _____1_____ with _____3_____.

A _____1_____ who _____4_____.

Fill the gaps with the following ideas:

1 the person's job (a farmer, a teacher), or their family relationship (an aunt, a cousin), or their relationship to you (neighbour, best friend)
2 something your character wears
3 something your character owns or carries
4 a favourite or regular activity (runs a sweetshop, buys large hats)
5 an adjective describing his/her character.

Examples a crazy hang-glider
an absent-minded maths teacher
a woman who runs the sweetshop
an aunt who came to live with us and wore headscarves
a young boy in army uniform
a farmer who left his farm once a year.

Pre-intermediate groups could be asked to select two or three key adjectives from a list suggested by you.

Examples exciting   interesting   clever   beautiful

talented   kind   brave   funny

5 After five minutes, ask your learners to write each of their descriptions on a blank label.

6 Now ask your learners to work with a partner. They should exchange their four labels with their partner. When every learner has their new set of labels, ask them to choose *one* of the characters on the label: the one that interests them most.

7 Now tell them they are going to write some sentences about the character on the label, underneath the character description. They should do so individually, without consulting their partner, and following your instructions.

Examples   **An aunt who came to live with us and wore headscarves**

Every day, she sang with her eyes closed.
She always carried with her a bag of sweets and an English dictionary.
Wherever she went, she tried to learn English words.
However, today was different, because this time she forgot her dictionary.

A young boy dressed in army uniform

Every day, he dreamt about the war.
He always carried with him a photograph of his beloved.
Wherever he went, he looked for her, here and there.
However, today was different, because this time he saw her in the street.

8 Read them the sentence openings below, and ask them to complete each sentence. Give the learners at least two minutes to finish each sentence. You might wish to add other sentence openings of your own.

Examples Every day, he/she _____.

He/she always carried with him/her _____.

Wherever he/she went, he/she always _____.

However, today was different, because this time _____.

9 When the learners have finished writing their labels, ask them to read these out in groups of four and discuss what might happen to their character next.

Variation 1

At step 6, it is also possible for learners to keep their own four character labels, and write sentences about the character from their own lives. This procedure works well if your learners have a preference for autobiography.

Homework

The learners could complete the story in five more sentences. These could be simple sentences using the past tense, as in the examples.

Comments

Typical errors are:

- omitting the relative pronoun, for example: *the woman runs the sweetshop*
- using tenses inconsistently. The verbs should be all in the past tense, OR all in the present tense. A typical error is to mix the two.

3.3 Heroes and villains: Delicia Darling and Molly Motherall

Many writers have tried to find the characters that all stories share. They have studied folk tales, myths, and popular stories, and indeed, there do seem to be character types which are common to all of these, and which are shared across cultures: heroes and villains, friends and mentors, fairy godmothers, teachers, and benefactors. This activity looks at these archetypal characters and how you can develop them in your story. There are more examples of character types in Appendix 2, page 162.

Level Intermediate and above

Elementary learners could do steps 1–3 of this activity.

Time 40 minutes

With the variation activities, this can be developed over two lessons.

Aims To work with adjectives to describe qualities admired and liked; to work with positive and negative connotation; to use the simple present for habitual actions/typical features; to consider the character types we find in stories and real life.

Procedure

1 Ask your learners to list people they admire, or could call their 'heroes' or 'role models'. Explain that they can think about real people in their lives, people in stories, famous people they have never met, or imaginary people. Learners who have done activity 3.2 could start with the characters they developed there. Write the names on the board. Discuss with your class.

- *Which of these are people you really know?*
- *Which of them are people you have only heard about through films, television, and newspapers?*

2 Now ask the learners to discuss with a partner why they have chosen these people.

Ask them to draw up together some of the key words to describe their 'heroes'.

With less advanced classes, you might want to write some possible adjectives on the board in advance, and ask your learners to choose the words that fit.

Examples famous
beautiful
rich
intelligent
kind
brave
friendly
motherly
sympathetic.

3 After five minutes, ask the learners to share their information with the class. Write any new words or ideas on the board.

4 Explain to the learners that they are now going to invent a new hero using the ideas on the board. Ask them to work in groups of two or three. They should:

a make up a new name for their 'hero' and complete the sentence below:

There once was a boy/girl/man/woman whose name was _____

b decide on his/her special qualities and complete the sentence below:

He/she was _____

c imagine those qualities are even more extreme—a kind person becomes saint-like, a brave person becomes superhuman in strength, a beautiful person becomes dazzling. Then, complete the sentence below:

He/she was, in fact, so ＿＿＿＿＿ (that) he/she ＿＿＿＿＿

Examples Allday Pies was so hospitable she stayed up all night baking cakes in case visitors came the next day.

Delicia Darling was so delicious she spent ten hours a day replying to love letters.

Molly Motherall was so sympathetic that people told her their problems all day long. She knew everybody's secrets.

d write four or five verbs describing the hero's everyday habits and actions. The verbs can be listed in the present tense to show regular everyday habits.

When dropped into the story, these verbs will need to be changed into the simple past, to be consistent with the rest of the story.

Example She stays calm, she always listens, she never gets angry, she smiles, she never talks about herself.

5 Now encourage the learners to develop the story, thinking about the consequences of having this special quality to such an extreme that it almost becomes a problem. Remind them to change the verbs into the simple past.

Example There once was a lady called Molly Motherall. She was so motherly that people were always telling her their problems. She spent so long listening kindly to problems that her face began to ache from smiling so much. People told her when they had money problems, love problems, work problems, housing problems, problems with teething babies, problems with their knees, and heart, and kidneys. All the time she smiled kindly. Then, one day, she fell down the stairs and broke her leg.

'I'd better not tell anyone, because they have so many problems of their own,' she thought.

All day she listened kindly to their problems, but by the end of the day she was fainting with pain.

'Are you all right?' her friend said.

'Oh yes!' she said, as she fainted on to the floor.

When she woke up, she was in her bed. There were crisp, clean sheets in the bed, and all round it, big bunches of flowers, a bowl full of grapes and peaches, a pile of juicy novels and magazines to read on a chair, a huge pot of tea in a new yellow teapot, and a card by her bed that said,

'To give is more blessed than to receive.'

Variation

This activity can be developed for other character types in stories. Follow the same procedure at each step, but change the opening instructions.

- Think about people we dislike/fear (villains).
- Think about best friends and 'fairy godmothers' (benefactors, donors, mentors).

Follow-up

It is interesting to note how often a quality can become a problem if exaggerated and taken too far. This can be a subject of discussion with your more advanced groups.

The learners can also imagine their heroes, villains, and best friends meeting one another.

- How does the villain make the hero's life difficult?
- How does the best friend help to resolve this difficulty?

3.4 Dressing your character: red shoes with roses

Level Elementary and above

Time 20 minutes

Aims To find ways to describe a character using items of clothing; to find ways to describe clothes: size, colour, texture, shape.

Procedure

1 Ask the learners to write down as many words for items of clothing as they can in 30 seconds. When they have finished, ask them to compare lists. Elicit their ideas and write as many on the board as you can.

2 Explain they are now going to make the items of clothing more specific, and imagine different story characters wearing each of them.

Example What kind of … shoes/hat/skirt/coat/shirt/trousers does your character wear?

How can we make these words more specific? Elicit and discuss with learners some of the categories below. They may also suggest others. An elementary class can work with the categories of colour and size. Intermediate and advanced classes can work with the other categories.

Examples colour
size: too big, too small, too short, too long
material: woolly, linen
shape: like a box, like a tank, like a pudding, like a pencil
texture: floppy, stiff, crisp
type of shoes: sandals, boots, stilettos, clogs

3   Ask the learners to choose a character from a story they have written, read about, or planned. Photos of people could also be used as a starting point, as well as clothes worn on another day/in another place. Ask them to 'dress' their character, being as specific as possible about each item of clothing. Encourage the learners to use a dictionary to build up further ways of making clothes specific.

Example   Delicia Darling: red stiletto heels with a rose on the ankle.

4   After five minutes, ask the learners to come up to the board and write the names of their characters there clearly.

5   Ask the learners to take it in turns to read their descriptions aloud to the class. Can the learners guess the name of their character from their clothes? You could turn this into a competition. The winner is the person who guesses the most names correctly.

Variation

Elementary learners could draw their characters' clothes. The learners could then match the name to the drawing. At a later step, the pictures could be labelled with the help of a dictionary.

President Featherhead

Delicia Darling

3.5 People talking: my spaceship is in your garden

In stories, things can 'happen' through conversations. This activity looks at conversations that are also 'events' in stories.

Level Intermediate and above

Time 30 minutes

Aims To work with synonyms of the verb *said*; to work with punctuation for dialogue; to practise reported speech.

Materials

One label per learner.

Preparation

Prepare the opening lines below on labels. There should be one label for each learner, so you will need to repeat some of these lines.

> Excuse me, that's my bag you've just picked up.

> Sorry, I can't let you in here dressed like that.

> I certainly DID pay for my ticket. Are you accusing me of lying?

> If you don't leave, I'm going to call the police.

> My spaceship is in your garden. My leader would like to meet you.

Procedure

1 Explain to the learners they are going to start 'stories' with conversations. Tell them they are going to work with a partner. Give each learner a label with one of the 'conversation lines'. Now ask them to take it in turns to read out their label to their partner, who should respond and continue the conversation until it reaches some kind of ending or conclusion.

2 The learners could now convert their conversation into a written story using reported speech. As preparation for this, ask the learners to use a dictionary or thesaurus to add further words to each of the lists below.

Examples

Synonyms of *said*	Synonyms of *replied*
commented	agreed
stated	answered
confirmed	echoed (to say the same thing
repeated (to say something again)	as the first speaker)
cried	responded
	retorted

You could also provide a model for the learners to show how a dialogue is punctuated.

Example 'If you don't leave, I'll call the police.'

'I think there must be a mistake. I am your long-lost cousin Brian,' he replied.

'Cousin Brian?!' she cried.

Variation

Choose one of the stories in this book. Give each learner a copy of the story. Ask them to choose a 'critical moment' or situation where the characters would have a conversation. Ask them to invent an 'opening line' for the conversation. These opening lines could be used as a starting point for this activity.

3.6 People searching: Delicia Darling's secret admirer

Level Intermediate and above

Time 40 minutes

Aim To use the infinitive structure; to use *but* clauses.

Preparation

Display or photocopy the two boxes on the next page.

Procedure

1 Give the learners two minutes to think about what they would put in each box and to write their ideas individually on a piece of paper. After two minutes, invite them to share their ideas with the class. Record these on the board, using the infinitive structure as below. This means each idea and object will need a verb. Ask the learners to help you formulate this structure once they have seen the pattern.

The reject box

Imagine a box where you can throw the things you don't want any more in your life.

They can be:

objects	thoughts
ideas	problems
habits	worries

Write down five of these to throw into the box.

The dream box

Imagine a box where you can store the things you most want in your life.

They can be:

objects	dreams
ideas	hopes for the
thoughts	future

Write down five of these to throw into the box.

Dream box	Reject box
to be rich	to be fat
to be famous	to be lazy
to go home	to listen to too loud music
to see my boyfriend/girlfriend	to be poor
to buy a car	to be clever
to learn English very well	to be shy
to fall in love	

2   Now ask your learners to choose one idea from the dream box and one from the reject box, and write a sentence using this frame:

(A name that you make up) *wanted* (dream idea), *but he/she* (reject idea).

Examples   *President Featherhead wanted to be rich but he was too lazy.*

Mungo the maths professor wanted to tell Delicia Darling he loved her, but he was too shy.

3   Ask your learners to form groups of two or three, and choose the sentence they find most interesting. They should consider the following questions:

- What can the character do to solve the problem?
- What does he/she do next?
- Does he/she succeed or not?

4   The answers will lead to a story. Ask the group to take notes as they plan the story. Then they could turn the story notes into other narrative types:

- an oral account, using the different voices of each person in the group
- a written story prepared by each learner for homework
- a story written by the group working together.

1 The characters in the activity above are searching for something they do not have. But in many stories, the reverse is true: characters try to get rid of something they *do* have, a fatal flaw or a personal quality that influences their lives negatively. Below are three characters with fatal flaws.

Examples *Struwwelpeter was so lazy he never cut his nails. His nails grew so long they arrived ten minutes before the rest of him.*

Mungo the professor was so messy he needed a ladder to climb over his papers.

Chelaka was so bad-tempered even the spiders ran away when she arrived.

2 Ask learners to write their own sentence choosing a character of their own. They can use the same sentence pattern as in the model. Then ask them to plan what happens because of this fatal flaw.

3.7 People changing: Don Foglio's camel

Level Elementary and above

Time 40 minutes

Aims To use adjectives and opposites; to use verbs that describe change.

Procedure

1 Write the following 'changes' on the board. You could also use examples of your own.

from poor to rich   from sad to happy   from child to adult

2 Ask your learners to suggest other ways in which people might change, and list these on the board.

from ugly to beautiful (and vice versa)
from fat to thin (and vice versa)
leaving home
changing jobs
from single to married (and vice versa)
from unemployed to employed (and vice versa)
from shy to confident.

3 Now ask your learners to work in groups of two or three. Ask them if they know a story, either real or fictional, in which people change in one of these ways. Ask them to tell their story to a partner. Elementary learners can do this step in their mother tongue.

4 Ask each group to choose the 'change' story they like best. Ask them to give the main character in the story a new name. Then ask them to complete the two sentences below and write them on a piece of paper.

At the beginning of the story, (name) …
At the end of the story, (name) …

Examples
- At the beginning of the story, Candy the sweetshop girl is very, very shy with no confidence.
- At the end of the story, Candy is a famous rock star.

- At the beginning of the story, Don Foglio lives on an industrial estate.
- At the end of the story, he is exploring the desert on a camel, and has grown a large moustache.

- At the beginning of the story, Chelaka was so bad-tempered that even the spiders ran away from her.
- At the end of the story, she was so kind and sweet that everyone thought she was ill.

5 Take in all the pieces of paper, shuffle them, and give one to each group. Ask each group to decide on the middle of the story.

How did the main character go from 1 to 2?
What happened in the middle?

Ask them to plan their stories and to take notes so they can give an oral account at the end of the lesson.

6 After 15 minutes, ask each group to tell their stories to the class. Ask the class to vote on the 'transformation' they think is:
- the most surprising
- the most amusing
- the most exciting.

Follow-up

As a follow-up, learners can turn their stories into written form, changing the present tense verbs into the past tense, and their notes into complete sentences. In the following lesson, they can use the editing checklists in Chapter 10 to improve one another's stories.

3.8 Inner and outer animals: the toad and the giraffe

This activity looks at the idea that we are all really two people: the person in our own mind that nobody can see but ourselves, and the person we present to the outside world and share with other people. What would happen if these two 'people' met? Would they fight, ignore each other, or become good friends?

Level Pre-intermediate and above

Time 30 minutes

Aims To look at vocabulary related to animals; to focus on adjectives used to describe contrasting qualities.

1 Ask your learners to think about:
   - the 'secret' person, hidden inside, that only they can see: what animal are you?
   - the person they are to the outside world that everyone can see: what is your outer animal?

2 Elicit some of their ideas and write them on the board.

Inside animals		Outside animals	
toad	monkey	giraffe	chipmunk
cat	lion cub	bulldog	lynx
secretive	lazy	open	lively
shy	dreamy	friendly	vivacious
quiet	calm	bubbly	crazy
thoughtful			

3 Ask your learners to work with a partner, and explain their two animals. Why have they chosen them? What is the difference between them?

Ask the partners to choose three adjectives to describe each of their animals. Above are some examples of contrasting adjectives.

Dictionaries or thesauri might be helpful for this activity.

Example Inside I am a toad, because I am very shy, very quiet and I do not wear bright clothes.

Outside I am a giraffe. I look very proud. I look very confident. I never get angry.

4 Now explain:
   - What if your two animals met one another one day?
   - What would they say? What would they think? What would they do?
   - Would they fight? If so, who would win?
   - Would they ignore one another?
   - Would they become friends?

Ask the partners to choose one of these three different plots: fight, ignore, or become friends?

5 Give the partners ten minutes to plan their story. They can:
   - write key words to show the different stages of the story
   - draw pictures to show different stages of the story
   - write the story out in full as they plan, editing, cutting, and expanding as they go along.

6 After ten minutes, ask partners to join with another pair and exchange their stories.

Follow-up

You could also set up specific ingredients you would like learners to include in their story. For example:

- include a conversation between the two animals.
- include a description of where they are when they meet.
- give your animals a name.

Variation

You may also suggest 'inner' and 'outer' people as follows:

- Think of your 'inner' person. Give him or her a name. Write three adjectives to describe him or her.
- Think of your 'outer' person. Give him or her a name. Write three adjectives to describe him or her.

The activity then continues at step 3 above.

Acknowledgements

This activity was planned with Rob Pope and tried out with Oxford Brookes teachers in June 2005.

4

A sense of place

This chapter looks at places in stories, not only as a background to the actions of the main characters, but as part of the story itself. Places have a great deal of character. In fact, they are sometimes as interesting as the people themselves. If we see a place vividly, we also smell, hear, and taste it. Real places, such as the sea, or the suburbs of a city, have moods, respond to changes, and react to traumas, just as people do.

This chapter looks at *place* as one of the key characters in a story: people in stories journey towards it, act within it and because of it. A place can jump up and act, play a key part in what happens, and give us a sense of a personality as important and dynamic as any played by the characters.

4.1 Comfort and discomfort zones: the elephant in the bus station

Level Elementary and above

Time 20 minutes

Aims To write descriptions of places using nouns, adverbs of place, adjectives of shape, size, and colour; to look at how people are affected by places.

Procedure

1 Write the chart on the next page on the board, choosing words your class will understand. If you have already used the activities in Chapter 3, you can use either some of the people and nicknames created by your own learners, or characters from stories that are familiar to them.

2 Elicit from learners more words for each of the boxes. If they run out of ideas, remind them of places and people in stories they have read, written, or heard about.

3 Now take as an example one of the characters in column 1 and model a question and answer.

People	Places
a gypsy	a library
a princess	the jungle
an astronaut	a high-rise/skyscraper
an old aunt in a headscarf	an industrial estate
a man from Mars	a bus station
an elephant	a betting shop
a long-distance lorry driver	a circus
a maths professor	a caravan
	a canoe

Example Where would your character feel most at home?

A gypsy would be most at home in a caravan.
A maths professor would be most at home in a library.

4 Ask the learners to work individually. They should select a character from the list (or from a story of their own), and decide on the place where their character is most at home.

5 Ask the learners to imagine they ARE that character, in their chosen place. They might want to close their eyes for two minutes to do this. After these two minutes, dictate the questions below one by one, giving the learners time between each question to write down an answer. You will find that the questions give a structure to the description.

a Are you inside or outside?
b Is it light or dark where you are?
c Is it hot or cold?
d What time of day/season of the year is it?
e Are you alone? Or with other people? If so, who else is there?
f Are there any animals, or insects, in this place? What are they? Do you like them?
g Is the place empty, or very full and crowded? With what, or with whom? Is it tidy or messy?
h What shapes and colours can you see?
i What sounds can you hear?
j What do you like best about this place?
k Do you have any special memories about this place?

6 If necessary, read the questions straight through, a second time. Then ask the learners to check their description, and see if there is anything else they would like to add.

7 After five minutes, ask each student to join a partner and to read or describe their place without mentioning the character. Ask partners to guess which character's 'comfort zone' or home is being described.

Variation 1: personal places

You could also ask the learners to consider the place where *they* are most at home, and then move straight to step 4 of this activity. At step 7, take in their written notes, shuffle them, and hand the descriptions out at random. The learners should then circulate and match the 'comfort zones' to their authors, by asking questions and talking to one another. This is an excellent teambuilding activity during the early stages of a class.

Variation 2: discomfort zones

A very fruitful variation consists in asking, at step 3, the question: *Where would your character feel **least** comfortable/at home?*

Examples
- a gypsy in a high-rise
- an old aunt in a canoe
- an elephant in the bus station.

To the questions at step 5 you could add others.

Examples What do you dislike most about being there?
How did you get there?

4. 2 People's rooms: Professor Mungo and the red straw hat

We can learn a lot about people by looking around the place where they live, at the photos on their walls, the objects they have kept from childhood, the gifts they have on their shelves that they choose to look at every day. These objects tell a story: a person who lives in a busy inland suburb has a collection of seashells; a person who lives in a basement flat has photos of the Himalayas around the walls.

Level Elementary and above

Time 20 minutes

Aims To look at the details inside a room; to look at objects that tell us about people.

Procedure

1 Ask the learners to think about a character in a story they have written, read, or heard about. Here are some of the names of characters in this book.

Example Delicia Darling
Mungo the professor
Molly Motherall
President Featherhead
Candy the sweetshop girl
Red Riding Hood
The Pied Piper.

2 Select one of these characters and ask your learners to think of three objects that might be found in the place where he/she lives.

3 Now show the learners the list in column A below. With elementary learners, you may want to adapt the chart to select key words and items they understand (furniture, books, colours, etc.) Ask them to add further ideas to the list.

Your character's room: Mungo the maths professor

A	B
the main colour in the room	brown: brown carpet, brown walls
furniture: size, shape, colour	a very large brown desk, with drawers all bursting open with papers
a natural object (stone, flower, etc.)	a very dry dead plant that he has forgotten to water, given as a gift from the librarian, who is secretly in love with him
anything that shouldn't be there?	a cobweb in the corner, with a large black spider
an object made, or repaired, by your character?	a pair of glasses stuck together in the middle with sticky-tape
an object left behind by a visitor?	a large red straw hat, left behind by the librarian (deliberately) on her last visit
a piece of clothing	a pile of unwashed socks in the corner of the room, with a crumpled shirt
food	bowl of milk left for the cat by the side of the door
a picture or photograph	black-and-white photo of a black-and-white cat
things stuck on the walls	a birthday card from the librarian saying 'To a special person'; another card saying 'Behind every talented person is a talented cat'
Any more ideas?	a book open on the desk, called Schroedinger's Cat

4 Ask the learners to work with a partner, completing the chart for a character of their own. The chart has been completed for Mungo the professor.

5 When the charts are completed, ask the learners to exchange with another group. With the new chart, ask the question:
What do you learn about the character from his/her room?

Mungo the professor likes cats better than people.

He is not at all interested in the librarian, who keeps giving him presents.

She wears brighter and brighter clothes, to make him notice her, but it is hopeless.

He is very untidy and disorganized.

He forgets to wash his clothes, water his plants, and tidy his room.

He loves Schroedinger, his cat.

He often feeds the cat, and forgets to feed himself.

Homework

Ask the learners to connect their notes into a coherent description. This could either be from the viewpoint of the character him/herself, or from the viewpoint of a visitor entering the room for the first time.

Variation

You could also ask the learners to think about their own room. They could then exchange their descriptions with a partner, and 'invent' a character who might inhabit their partner's room.

4.3 Five senses: the empty bus station

This activity invites you to think about the five senses, and how they can be used to give a clear description of a place.

Level Pre-intermediate and above

Time 20 minutes

Aim To use vocabulary related to the five senses; to build descriptions of places; to edit texts from first to third person.

Procedure

1 Draw the boxes below on the board. Elicit from your class some words describing what they can see, hear, taste, smell, and touch in the place where they are now, and write it into each box.

I can see	I can hear	I can smell
	I can taste	I can touch

2   Now ask your learners to work individually filling in the boxes with the sensations they experience when they go on a journey they know well. It could be a regular journey to visit a friend or member of their family. Give them five minutes to write as many words as they can in each of the boxes. They should write the words clearly, because they will be read by another student.

3   After five minutes, ask the learners to work in groups of two or three, and exchange their list of words with a partner.

4   Ask each learner to describe their partner's scene orally, using the words on the list.

They can describe the scene using the pronoun: *you*, or imagine it is their own experience, and use the pronoun *I*.

5   Now ask each learner to write a short description of the place on their partner's list that they have already described orally. This time, ask them to use the pronoun: *he/she*. The 'person' they are describing is no longer their partner, but a new, fictional character they can imagine for themselves.

- He was sitting alone in a bus station.
- It was very early in the morning, and still dark.
- He could hear the cars in the street outside.
- He could smell torn fish and chip wrappers thrown onto the floor.
- But he could not see a bus. Though he waited, and waited, and waited, no bus arrived.

6   After ten minutes, ask partners to share their descriptions. With a more advanced class, you could discuss the following questions:

- Is the 'new' scene the same as the one first imagined?
- What is the effect of changing the pronoun?
- Who could the 'he' or 'she' now be?
- Can you give this new character a name?
- What is going to happen next in this setting?

Homework

Ask your learners to tell the story of 'what happens next' and bring this to share in the next lesson.

4.4 Journey to Freeland

Level   Pre-intermediate and above

Time   20 minutes

Aim   To use verbs of travel and adverbial phrases to describe the manner of travel; to practise the use of discourse markers for chronological sequence; to listen for sequence and detail.

Procedure

1   Write the word QUEST on the board.

Explain that a quest is a journey to find someone or something magical or life changing. Below is a list of possible reasons for quests. Can they suggest others?

> **Quest**
>
> to find eternal youth
>
> to find perfect love
>
> to find the meaning of life
>
> to find the crystal ball that explains the future

2 Tell your learners they are going to imagine travelling to ONE of these places from where they are sitting now, in the classroom.

Where would they choose to go?

3 If this is practical, ask all the students with the same choice of journey, to work together. Otherwise, divide the class into groups of two or three at random. Explain that each group is going to imagine the journey, or quest, to their chosen place.

4 Build up with your class ideas to describe their journey. The blackboard chart below is a possible frame. Ask the students to suggest words for each of the columns.

Places	Prepositions and adverbs	Ways of travelling	Verbs of movement
mountain	up/down	by boat	walk
tunnel	along	by bus	trudge
cave	through	by scooter	crawl
beach	around	by lorry	hike
canal	on	on a skateboard	saunter
subway	in	on a donkey	whizz
river	out	on horseback	run
suburb	about	in a cart	fly
dockland		on a sledge	sail
		by train	cycle
		by lorry	
		on foot	

5 Ask groups to describe their journey. They should move through at least three different places and using at least three different ways of travelling. The starting point should be the classroom. As they plan, one person in the group should write short notes.

6 After 15 minutes, ask each group to describe their quest to the class.

Follow-up

Learners could now work together to write down the journey as a coherent description. The sequencing words below may help to connect the different stages of the journey.

- first
- then
- hours/days/weeks later
- after that
- after a long while
- finally.

Variation

While they listen to their partner's journey, the learners could also draw a 'travel line' in the form of a diagram, a picture, a chart, or a set of labels along a line to illustrate their journey. Specific time references could be added to the line at a later stage.

Example Journey to the land of no study.

FREELAND

CAVES OF FREELAND

FREEBODY FIELD

FORGETITALL LAKE

RUNAWAY FOREST

SCHOOL

4.5 Changing time zones: Blue Denim and the security guard

Level Intermediate and above

Time 20 minutes

Aims To use vocabulary to describe objects at different periods of time; to contrast time frames: past and present.

Procedure

1 Choose a story your learners are familiar with. Any story will work with this activity, including traditional tales and local stories known in your classroom. The examples used in this activity will be from the tale of Little Red Riding Hood. Tell the story to your class.

2 Ask your learners:
   - When does the story take place?
   - Is it today?
   - Is it set in the past?
   - How do you know?

   Below are some possible answers:

   clothing: red riding hoods are not worn today
   objects: she may not use a basket nowadays to carry her shopping
   food: Grandma might want something more substantial than cherries
   customs: walking through the forest alone wouldn't be encouraged today
   travel: if it was a long way she probably wouldn't walk
   jobs people do: the job of 'woodcutter' doesn't really exist any more. He would be called a 'tree surgeon'.
   language: a modern child would probably not say 'Oh, Grandmother'

3 Now explain you are going to change the time setting of the story. What if Little Red Riding Hood was dropped into the 21st century? What would need to change?

   Elicit ideas from the class using the categories at step 2 to help:

   clothing: she would wear jeans and a T-shirt
   objects/food: she would carry some microwave food in a rucksack
   customs/travel: she would order a cab to Grandma's using her mobile phone
   jobs people do: she would be saved by the security guard at Grandma's block of flats
   language: she would call Grandma 'Gran' or 'Nan'.

4 When the class has shared several ideas about changes, ask them to work in groups of two or three, and rewrite the story as set in modern times, using ideas of their own.

They could share ideas orally in class, and write them as coherent stories for homework.

Follow-up

When the learners have finished their stories, invite them to share with a neighbour and compare the ways they have made the story 'modern'.

Variation

The opposite time change could also be practised. A 'modern' story, such as the life of a celebrity or a soap-opera story, could be dropped into prehistoric times or into a historic period of time.

5

Something happened

We saw in Chapter 1 that a story where the main character begins at the beginning and ends at the end, with no problems in between, is really no story at all. Action alone might be interesting, but a story needs to take us a little further. The main character needs to change a little, learn something new, end up in a different place from where he or she started, or we, the readers, need to change a little, learn something new. What is it that makes this change happen?

Many readers and storytellers over the centuries have tried to find the 'key to all stories': the story ideas that are universal to all cultures and all peoples at all times. In 3.3 we met character types that are found in many stories around the world. In this chapter, we will look at some plot types which people have thought are at the centre of all stories: journeys, loss and separation from home, battles against danger, trials and tests, returns from long absences, and reconciliation between opponents.

Below is a list of ways you can make a story 'grow', once you have a character (see Chapter 3) and a place (see Chapter 4). Of course, most stories make things 'happen' in several of these ways at the same time. These 'ingredients' can be combined in any way that gives the storyteller the richest mixture and the most fertile soil for finding their own story.

- Give your character an object or person to seek and take him/her on a long journey (activity 5.1)
- Make your character discover something that changes everything (activity 5.2)
- Make your character leave home for the first time (activity 5.3)
- Make your character arrive at a place that is new, strange, or extraordinary (activity 5.4)
- Introduce a character into the story that makes life difficult for him/her
- Introduce a battle your character must win.
- Introduce a prize your character longs for, but which is difficult to win (most love stories), such as the one at the start of Chapter 7
- Introduce a difficult choice for the main character. Show how/what he/she decides, why, and what the consequences are (activity 5.5)
- Make your character return home after a long journey which has changed him/her (activity 5.6)
- Ask a question about the world (activity 5.7)

In the appendix, there is a checklist of story archetypes that can be used as the basis for an infinite number of further story ideas.

5.1 The quest: the shepherd and the pyramids

Level Pre-intermediate and above

Time 20 minutes

Aims To work with questions and answers; to work with adverbial phrases of place (*over*, *under*, *across* etc.); to use *because* clauses; to predict the last line.

Procedure

> There was a shepherd who had a strange and wonderful dream. In his dream, he saw an old man sitting under the Egyptian pyramids. The old man told him that he would find a wonderful pot of gold that would make him rich and happy forever. But only by visiting the pyramids would the shepherd learn where this pot of gold was hidden. So the shepherd sold all his sheep and went on a long, long journey across the sea, over the mountains, across the desert, through hills and valleys, to find the old man.
>
> Sure enough, as in his dream, he found the wise man sitting at the foot of the pyramids.
>
> 'Tell me, oh wise man, where is the pot of gold that was in my dream?'
>
> 'The pot of gold is under your bed at home. Your wife hid it there while you were asleep.'
>
> 'But, oh wise man, why have I travelled all this way simply to find out that the gold is under my own bed? Why did you appear to me in a dream to tell me that?'

1 Tell, or read aloud, the story above to your learners. You could change the underlined words to use scenes, or places, or objects that are familiar to your learners.

2 Ask your learners to finish the story by suggesting what the wise man's answer might be. In this version, the wise man says: 'Because without this dream, you would never have seen the Egyptian pyramids.'

Elicit your learners' ideas for the wise man's reply. Here are some replies suggested by learners:
- because you never really liked your wife but now you will!
- because you had a good holiday
- because you will be happy now with what you have
- because you should never trust dreams, but real life instead.

3 Ask your learners to choose the answer they like best, and to explain why.

4   When the learners have selected their ending, ask them to develop their own version of the story. Explain to them that they can do several things with it.
   - They can change the object being looked for.
   - They can change the main character to someone young/old, a man/woman.
   - They can give him/her a name.
   - They can describe the journey.
   - They can change the wise man to another character type.
   - They can change the question and answer.

Choose whether you would like this version:
   - to be developed orally
   - to be developed orally with one learner taking notes
   - to be developed orally at first, with the group then creating a written version using their notes.

Variation

Tell the story and pause where the words are underlined. Ask your learners to 'fill in the gaps' with their own ideas. Ask them to say their suggestions out loud, and add them to your story.

This story is a synopsis of the novel *The Alchemist*, by Paolo Coelho.

5.2 Stories about loss: the disappearing song

Level   Elementary and above

Time   20 minutes

Aims   To use modals for speculation; to work at completing a story; to work at interpreting a story.

Procedure

1   Tell the class this story. You could either read it aloud using the words as they are here, or develop it in your own way to match the level of the group.

There once was a man who loved the sound of birdsong. Every day he went to the forest to hear the birds. He listened, and listened, and listened. The songs were so beautiful that all day he sang them to himself. When he worked, and ate, and went to sleep, he heard in his mind the songs of the birds.

But one day, he went into the forest and the birds were no longer singing. He waited, and waited, and waited, but still he couldn't hear the song of the birds. There was only silence: a long and terrible silence.

---

2 Ask your learners the following questions:

- *What do you think has happened?*
- *Why are the birds no longer singing?*
- *Where are the birds?*
- *What has happened to them?*

Ask your learners to answer the questions, using the phrases on the blackboard charts below.

You can choose the chart that suits the level of your learners best.

Chart 1: Modal verbs

The birds	might may could	be have
They		

Chart 2: Adverbs for speculation

Maybe	they	have
Perhaps	the birds	
Possibly		

3 Now continue the story by eliciting ideas about what happens next.

- What does the man feel?
- What does the man do next?
- Does he try to find the birds? If so, how? And where?
- Why do you think the birdsong was so important to the man?
- Do you think this story is about the real world? If so, how?

4 Ask the class to work in groups of two or three to answer the questions on the board. They could:

- plan their answers orally, with one learner in each group making notes as a memory aid
- have each learner take notes, so they can write the story in full for homework.

5 After ten minutes, ask each group to report back on some of their ideas. They could:

- tell the story
- mime the story, with a commentary from one narrator in the group
- mime the story without narration.

Variation 1

Ask your learners to find a 'meaning' for the story. What do they think it is *really* about?

Is it a metaphor for the disappearance of a people, a language, a culture?

Or is it about the psychology of the main character or the changing ecology of the forest?

Variation 2

It could also be a story about being separated from somebody/something admired or loved. Ask learners to change 'birdsong' to somebody/something else. It could be a person, a place, an animal, or an object. Then follow the same procedure.

5.3 Stories about leaving home

Some of the most loved children's stories are about children leaving home and meeting the dangers of the outside world. This could be considered as a 'rite of passage', something everyone has to go through in the passage from childhood to adulthood.

Level Intermediate and above

Time 30 minutes

Aims To contrast the use of *would* for dreams and hopes in the past with that of the simple past for actual events; to convert notes in the present simple into the simple past for narratives.

Procedure

1 Read or tell the story below. Change the names to make them typical of names in your context. You could also change 'son' to 'daughter'. Make the changes your learners will most identify with.

> *Inderjit* and *Sumi* were so proud! Their *son* was going to university in the city. He was the first in the family to go away to study. He was very clever. He could be a doctor, or an engineer, or anything he wanted. He would become rich, and buy a large house in the city, and they would go to visit. He would have lots of famous and rich friends, and would be invited all over the world. Wherever he went, Inderjit and Sumi would go and visit. They were so excited about the new life for their son—and the new life for them too!

2 Ask the learners to work in groups of two or three. Ask them each of the following questions one at a time. Give the groups five minutes to talk about each one.

   - Give the son/daughter a name.
   - What does he/she think about the journey to the university?
   - Does he/she have the same hopes as Inderjit and Sumi?
   - Will these hopes be fulfilled or not? Decide what happens to your character when he/she arrives in the city.
   - Are the parents happy or not? What do they do next?

3 Ask the groups to write brief notes in answer to these questions. These can be short sentences using the present simple, or even short words and phrases.

Examples Yes, her hopes are fulfilled. After a lot of hard work, she becomes a doctor. She returns to the village and sets up a clinic for sick babies. She is the first doctor ever to work in the village. But her parents are very worried, because she is so clever none of the local men want to marry her.

He doesn't want to become a doctor or engineer at all. He wants to be a musician. When he arrives in the city, he finds a singer and a drummer, and they set up a rock band. His parents are furious and refuse to speak to him or send him any money. He leaves college and gets a job in a cafe to try and make money.

When he goes to college, he finds the work very difficult. He just can't understand the lessons, and fails all his exams. He is too afraid to tell his parents, so he stops writing to them. They are very worried, and send an uncle to the city to find him.

4 The learners can either keep their own notes from step 3, or you could ask them to exchange their notes with those of another group, so each group has a new set of ideas. Ask each group to combine their notes into a story. Encourage them to use modal verb forms.

Examples • *would* to describe all the hopes of the parents
• *would* or *will* to describe all the hopes of the main character: 'I'll join a band! I'll play the guitar!'
• simple past to describe the events that happened next.

5 After 15 minutes, when all the synopses have been written, ask the learners for a show of hands to answer some questions about the story.

Examples *How many of you wrote stories with a happy ending?*
How many of you wrote stories with a sad ending?
How many of you wrote stories with neither a happy nor a sad ending?

6 Ask each group to tell their story. It can be told orally, or read from the written version. Ask the class to vote which story they like best.

7 A more advanced class may like to discuss the differences between the stories and what we learn about the main character and his/her family in each.

Variation

The story at the start of this activity can be changed using many different kinds of 'leavings'. You could start the activity by brainstorming reasons for leaving home. They could then choose one of these, and work through the activities as above.

leaving home for the first time	to study at university to get married to become a soldier to get a job in the city to escape the war to learn a language in a foreign country to visit a relation to sing in a concert

5.4 Stories about arrival: Bran's desert island

Every traveller needs to arrive somewhere in the end. For every leaving, there is an arrival. Many great stories describe the arrival of a traveller in a strange and unknown place. Gulliver arrives in places where all the people are either very tiny or big as giants. The Lotus Eaters arrive at an island that makes them forget their homeland.

Level Intermediate and above

Time 30 minutes

Aims To describe first impressions; to describe places.

Procedure

1 Read or tell the story below.

> Bran, the fisherman, was tired of the seas where he fished every day.
>   So one day, he put his sail against the wind and sailed, and sailed away from the cold grey coast where he lived. He sailed until he came to a small island with golden sands. Along the sands were wonderful trees heavy with coconuts, pineapples, and bananas. He pulled his boat onto the shore, and sat under the banana tree to eat.
>   It was so wonderful on the island that he stayed, and stayed. Days went by, then weeks, then months. Then, suddenly he thought, 'My dear mother, and father, and sister, and brother, and the girl I love! How I miss them!'
>   So he ran to find his boat, but there was no boat to be found. And he ran to find a bridge over the sea, but no bridge was to be found. Then a voice said, 'Once you have found me, you can never turn back.'

2 Ask the learners to change the underlined words in the first two sentences, using ideas of their own. They should write two new sentences on a piece of paper.

Examples Fayed the jeweller was tired of the shop where he worked every day. So one day, he caught the bus to Delhi from the corner by the sweetshop, and rode away from the streets where he lived.

CheeAi the housewife was tired of the kitchen where she cooked every day. So one day, she walked away from the kitchen where she lived, and went to the ocean, to see the sea.

3 Ask the learners to work in groups of two or three. Ask them to choose the scene that interests them the most. They should understand that the place could be anywhere.

Examples • a fantasy place, like the moon or the Centre of the Earth
• a real place you know very well
• a real place you have never visited.

4 Ask them to describe what happens when the main character arrives at the distant place. Guide them with questions if necessary.

Examples What does he/she see?
Who does he/she meet?
Is it possible to turn back?

5 With a more advanced class, learners may enjoy discussing what the last line means: *Once you have found me, you can never turn back.*

Examples Is this literal or is it about personal change?
Is it true that a journey can change you so you 'can never turn back'?
Do the characters in the learners' stories change in this way?

Follow-up

Learners could use the activities in Chapter 4 to help them develop the place where they arrive.

5.5 Difficult choices: Dino's dilemma

Level Intermediate and above

Pre-intermediate learners can do steps 1 and 2 of the activity.

Time 20 minutes

Aims To work at establishing contrasts: *on the one hand/on the other hand…*; to work at comparing and contrasting.

Procedure

1 Tell or read the learners the story on the next page.

Dino's dilemma

There once was a young man called Dino, who had a terrible problem. There were two women who loved him, and he couldn't choose between them. One of them was very kind, and good, and wise. Every time Dino talked to her, he learnt more about the world. But she was so ugly he preferred to talk to her in the dark. She was very old, and bent, and she had very large ears, and hair on the back of her hands. The other woman was so beautiful every man who saw her fainted with love. She was graceful, and had golden hair like silk, and skin like velvet. However, she was so stupid, and selfish, and unkind she made him weep every day. Sometimes, he was so angry and unhappy he thought he would die. But he had to choose between the two women. So he went to the philosopher.

'What should I do? One is so wise, I feel like a god with her, but she is so ugly I dare not look at her. One is so cruel, I feel like a worm with her, but she is so beautiful I almost faint with love. Oh philosopher! Which is more important: beauty or wisdom?'

The philosopher thought a little, then said, 'First make your choice. Then, from your choice, you will know which is the more important.'

2 Ask questions about the story and elicit responses.
- *What do you think the young man should do?*
- *Was the philosopher's advice helpful or unhelpful?*
- *What would you have said to the young man?*

3 Now divide the class into two halves and give them instructions about possible follow-ups for the story.

Example GROUP A: Imagine that the young man marries the wise woman. Plan the story of the first year after their marriage.

GROUP B: Imagine that the young man marries the beautiful woman. Plan the story of the first year after the marriage.

4 After ten minutes, ask the groups to report back on their stories. Then invite the class to vote on which was the best choice for the young man.

Variation

This procedure can be used to explore other stories involving choices. Ask the learners to write their own 'choices' stories.

5.6 The return of the hero: Oscar's problem

Level Intermediate and above

Time 30 minutes

Aims To work at contrasting *would* for speculation with *would* for habit in the past for actual events; to work at contrasting different characters' viewpoints.

Procedure

1 Read or tell the story opening below. You could use names your learners are familiar with in place of those in the story.

Oscar was only four years old, but he felt like a grown-up. He was the only man in the house. Oscar would help his mother to cook, he would go shopping with her, and he would stand beside her jealously when other men talked to her.

However, one day, a tall man with large boots arrived at the house. Oscar was surprised to see his mother kissing and hugging him.

'This is your father, Oscar', she said. 'Isn't it lovely he's home at last! Oh, I'm so happy!'

Oscar couldn't understand why she was crying if she was so happy. He also thought it very unfair that his Mother insisted on kissing this man all the time.

Later that day, he met Father in the corridor on his way to the kitchen. Oscar stood in front of the door to stop him going in.

'You aren't allowed', he said to the man, who had now taken off his large boots.

'I know it's your own special home here', the man said, 'but, you know, it's my special home too and all three of us have to share it now.'

---

2 Ask your learners: *Where do you think Oscar's father has been?* Write their suggestions on the board.

Examples at war
working in the city
building a city in the desert
looking for their elder son who is lost
just recovered his memory after an accident.

3 Invite the class to choose one of the possibilities from the list.

4 Ask the learners to divide into three groups. Allocate to each group one of the viewpoints below. Ask each group to write notes in answer to your questions.

Examples   GROUP 1: Tell the story from the mother's point of view:
What would she feel?
GROUP 2: Tell the story from Oscar's point of view:
Do you think Oscar will grow to accept his father?
GROUP 3: Tell the story from the husband's point of view:
Have his experiences changed him? How?

5   After ten minutes, ask each group to share their stories. A story of return, from different points of view, will emerge from these three groups. The learners share the stories orally.

Follow-up

The learners could prepare a written version of the story, choosing one of the three viewpoints they have shared.

Variation

Ask the learners to choose other situations in which someone returns home after a long absence. Ask them to tell the story of the return, from two different points of view.

5.7 Questions about the world: Kraon the thunder god

Many stories have been created to answer questions about the world, or experiences that have distressed people. For example, many myths answer questions about how the world was created, or why a flood happened, or where death came from. Even though the answers to these questions are not 'scientific', they fulfil an important function for the storyteller and listener: they allow us to voice questions that seem too big to answer, and they give us a sense of resolution and safety when we try to answer them.

Level   Elementary and above

Time   20–40 minutes

Aims   To use the simple past; to organize information in a narrative sequence; to transfer short notes and key words into complete paragraphs.

Procedure

1   Write this phrase on the board and ask your learners to complete it. Explain they can make their sentence as long or as short as they like.

I wonder why …

Examples   I wonder why there needs to be jealousy.
I wonder why we always have wars.
I wonder why we have to work so hard.
I wonder why we speak so many languages.
I wonder why it rains so much.

2   Ask the class if any of them know stories that give answers to these questions. Ask them to tell them to the class.

Examples *The story of Pandora's box*
The story of the Garden of Eden
The Machu Pichu story

3 Ask the class if they notice anything special or surprising about these stories. You might like to share with them some of the ideas below.

> There is no specific time or place.
>
> The characters are not real people whose names we recognize.
>
> The 'answers' do not pretend to be historical, factual, or scientific.
>
> There is often a magic object, such as an apple, or a box.
>
> Abstract ideas, such as 'knowledge', or 'evil', are made concrete: they exist in boxes or apples.

Write these points on the board as you discuss them, along with other ideas from the group.

4 Divide the class in groups of three or four and ask each group to choose one of the sentences from step 1, or invent another one of their own. When they have done so, ask them to listen to the following questions, and individually write one or two words or short phrases in answer to each one.

> Who is the main character in your story? Write down his/her name.
>
> When did he/she live?
>
> Where did he/she live?
>
> What did he/she do before this thing came to the world?
>
> Your character became unhappy and wanted change. Why?
>
> What did your character do as a result?
>
> Your character finds this object. How?
>
> What did he/she do next?
>
> By mistake, your character lets this object out into the world. How?

5 When you have finished reading the questions and the learners have had time to answer them, ask them to compare their answers in their groups, and to choose the best answers.

6 The group's task will now be to write a short synopsis of their story, using the information they have chosen. Ask them to expand their key words or phrases into complete sentences, using the simple past, and the following opening and closing sentences.

Example   Once upon a time there was a _____ called

_____.

_____ (something happened)

And that is why _____.

Encourage them, also, to use the information in the same order as their notes.

Below are some examples of how students transferred their notes into a connected paragraph.

Why there have to be wars

Kraon, god of thunder

At the beginning of time

In the sky

Played with thunder

Lonely in the sky

Came down to earth

Tries to make thunder down there, bangs, crashes, loud noises

No good, so he made guns and bombs

People on earth wanted to try out the guns and bombs too

Once upon a time, there was a large god who made thunder, called Kraon.

He lived in the sky, at the beginning of time.

He played with thunder. He made loud noises and rolled stones around the sky.

But he was lonely in the sky, so he decided to come down to earth.

On earth he tried to make thunder. He tried bangs, crashes, but they were no good. It was better in the sky.

So he thought, 'What shall I do?'

Then he made guns and bombs that were like the thunder.

People on earth saw this. They wanted to try out the guns and bombs too. Also, they were jealous and angry. They began to fight for the guns.

And that is why wars came to the earth.

Follow-up 1

As a follow-up, learners could choose another question and write their own synopsis, using their notes and the order of information in their class stories, to help them.

Follow-up 2

Use the ideas in Chapter 9 to encourage learners to share and develop their stories with others, orally. The stories could also be collected into a class anthology. See ideas in Chapter 10 for editing and polishing the written versions of the story.

Variation

This activity can also work with pre-intermediate learners. To do so, give them sentences to complete.

> Once upon a time there was a _____
>
> He/she lived in _____
>
> Most of the time he/she was very happy. Every day he/she would _____
>
> However, one day something changed. Suddenly he/she felt unhappy, because _____

Photocopiable © Oxford University Press

Acknowledgements

The story *Why there have to be wars* was developed by Japanese learners, with the participation of an interpreter at Oxford Brookes, summer 2003.

6
Pattern stories

This chapter looks at the idea of building stories through language patterns. Although this works very well with elementary learners, the qualities of these stories are as effective with adults as with children. They include the qualities of repetition, chant-like refrains, and patterns. They also include the use of language structures as building blocks for stories. Through these patterns, learners can enjoy both the pleasure of listening to a story, and the challenge of helping to build it. These are also amongst those rare activities that work even better with large classes.

Reading-aloud tip for the teacher

Some of these stories deliberately play with long, expanding sentences. The story and sentence types should be read with a steady rhythm. This means that as the sentences become longer, you can read them faster and faster to fit the rhythm. You could 'beat time', just like a beat in music, so learners speak together and the choral reading does not become 'ragged'.

6.1 Substitution story: the invisible people

Level Elementary and above

Time 20 minutes

Aims To build stories using sentence frames; to work with *would/used to* for regular habits in the past; to expand sentences with modifying phrases.

Procedure

1 Copy the following chart on to the board. You can choose which words or phrases to write in columns 2 and 4. Add further ideas that you know your class are familiar with.

2 Ask your class to look at the chart and suggest further ideas to go into each of the boxes. Write some of their ideas on the board.

3 Now ask your learners, either individually or in pairs, to suggest the two sentences following on from the chart. They can be phrases, or gap sentences like the ones already on the board. Elicit some examples after five minutes, and write these on the board.

1	2	3	4
There once was a	princess soldier schoolboy housewife businessman shopkeeper fisherman little boy	who lived	in a castle in a bedsit in a cupboard in a skyscraper under a bridge on an industrial estate on the railway sidings (by the side of the railway)
Every day he/she would	walk go listen to visit think about send a message to		
But one day, he/she	decided to thought he/she would		
On the way, he/she met	a little boy an old man …	who was	
The (other character) said			
and he/she replied			

Examples *Both of them were very …*
Immediately, he/she …
He/she was so … that he …

4 Now ask them to work in groups of two or three to build a story using the frame.

Example There once was a businessman who lived in a skyscraper and drove to work.

Every morning, he would go twenty floors down in the lift to go to work. At night he would go twenty floors up again. Every day he went up and down, until he felt like an aeroplane.

But one day, he thought it would be interesting to live somewhere near the ground. So, he decided to go and look at other places. On his walk, he met a little boy who was very dirty and wore no shoes. The little boy said, 'Can you give me some money?'

'I will, if you take me to your home and show me where you live,' the businessman replied.

'Certainly,' the little boy said. He took the businessman on a short walk to the railway station.

'This is the railway station!' said the businessman.

'Yes, and that's where I live.' The little boy pointed. On the side of the railway were rows and rows of houses made of boxes and pieces of cardboard. Some had television aerials sticking out of them. Some had washing lines hung between the telegraph poles.

'All these years, and I never noticed these homes,' he said to the little boy.

'Yes,' the little boy said. 'They call us the invisible people.'

'Mmm…,' the businessman thought. 'Perhaps it's not so bad living on top of a skyscraper after all.'

5 After ten minutes, ask the learners to share their stories. There are several possible procedures.
   • joining with another group and reading their stories aloud
   • putting their stories on the wall, and moving round the room reading one another's
   • miming the story.

6.2 Expanding sentence story: five children, two cats, a goat, and three cows

Level Elementary and above

Time 20 minutes

Aims To look at how a sentence can be expanded; to expand verb phrases of the type: *she had to + verb*; to use vocabulary for household chores; to listen for detail.

Procedure

1 Tell or read this story aloud to your class. As you reach each underlined part, read one or two examples only and invite your class to suggest further ones. Repeat their suggestions so they become part of the story. You can also 'improvise' this story by using your own ideas to change and add to each part.

2 Now ask the learners to finish the story, using the ideas they have invented.

Variation

There are other stories in this book you could also use as expanding stories, for example, activity 1.5 ('Changing places', in which a husband and wife exchange their tasks on a typical day) or activity 2.8 ('The king's dinner', in which learners could increase the number of people and animals in the king's entourage, the amount of food and drink they consume, and the mess they leave behind).

There once was a woman who was very tired.
  She lived with <u>five children, her husband, her husband's brother, ...</u> *(add animals, family members, neighbours, friends).*

Every day, she had to <u>clean the house, make the beds, do the shopping, chop the wood for the fire, ...</u> *(add household jobs).*
  One day, she decided, 'I've had enough! I'm going to change everything! I'm going to ask <u>my husband to clean the house and make the beds, my eldest son to chop the wood, and my eldest daughter to chop the vegetables, peel the potatoes, and cook the meal, and ...</u> *(delegate the jobs to friends and family: see if learners can remember their suggestions from the first two sentences).*

So she said to them, '<u>Husband, Daughter, Son, Brother in-law, Sister in-law</u>, it's your turn to do the jobs in the house. I am going to sit by the fire and have a rest. You have plenty of time. I am in no hurry. I'll sit by the fire and give you advice.

<u>So the husband cleaned the house, and the eldest son chopped the wood, and the eldest daughter chopped the vegetables</u> ...
(See if learners can remember which jobs went to which family member.)

Comments

The words suggested by learners should all be of the same type as your first example.

Examples SENTENCE 1: all nouns. Two of the gaps are specifically family members, but the gap can be filled with neighbours, friends, or animals.

SENTENCE 2: all verbs in root form. The suggestions are all household jobs, but learners might expand the ideas to include other things the character does in a typical day.

6.3 Sentence type stories: Croak's table

Some writers draw their stories from fragments of conversations, pictures, images, and fleeting visual snapshots. Here is a framework that can be used in the language class, which at the same time practises four different sentence types.

Level **Pre-intermediate and above**

Time **40 minutes**

Aim **To practise patterns of four sentence types: exclamation, question, command, and statement; to use sentence types as a starting point for building stories.**

Procedure

1 Draw four boxes on the board, and write two or three examples of your own in each box. Invite your learners to add more examples to each box.

Questions	Exclamations
What are these strange marks?	Rose, you are so red!
How did you get here?	Never!
Why are you blushing?	No!
What is this fork doing in the lamplight?	Help!
Why is the pot empty?	
Who owned this table before we did?	
Statements	**Commands**
His/her name is ...	Run quickly!
The reason is ...	Get well soon!
The answer is ...	Please, tell me.
It was true, he/she ...	Don't do that!
He/she said ...	Stop now!
	Go home!

2 Ask your learners to work in groups. They should select one line from each box and connect them into one story. They can use as many sentences and ideas as they like, but they should join each of the ideas into a coherent story.

Example 'What are these strange marks on the table? Someone has carved a name in the wood.'
'Yes! It says CROAK.'
'Oh, no!'
'Why did you say that?'
'Because today I found a note under the door. It said: "I will find you wherever you are. Croak."'
'It can't be true. Jerome Croak lived in this house 200 years ago.'
'Oh, goodness! What shall I do?'
'Go home. I will talk to him tonight.'
'Talk to him! How?!'
'I can't tell you now. Wait for me tomorrow under the apple tree. Then I will explain everything.'

Variation

For less advanced learners, you could use one of these sentence types at a time.

Example **Exclamations**
Add as many exclamations as you can to the box.
Now write a story, using the exclamations to help you.
Oh no!
Yes!
Never!
Yes!

Follow-up

You could spend time with the class, looking at the verb form in each of the boxes at step 1. Learners could work out their own rules for each box.

Examples   EXCLAMATIONS: often no verb at all. Short phrases, sounds, or single words.

COMMANDS: the verb is in the root form, with no changes for person or time.

QUESTIONS: the verb and the person change places: 'Are you?!' OR the auxiliary 'do' goes at the front of the question: 'Do you know what this is?'

6.4 Beginning-of-time stories: the sky people

Level   Pre-intermediate and above

Time   20 minutes

Aims   To use *could/couldn't* to describe physical abilities; to use vocabulary for animals and landscape; to develop the middle of a story.

Procedure

1   Read, or tell, the story on the next page to your learners. This is an American Indian creation myth, but the learners are going to invent their own middle to the story. When you reach the underlined parts, ask the learners to add their own suggestions. They should use the same form as you: the root of the verb.

2   Explain that the middle part of the story is missing. Ask the learners to work in groups of two or three and write the middle part by answering the question:

• How did the sky people come to live on earth?

3   After ten minutes ask the learners to mime their story, or tell it to another group.

Follow-up 1

Children could write their version of the story, either individually, or in pairs for homework.

Follow-up 2

A more advanced group might be interested in discussing what views of the earth, the environment, and nature is revealed by their suggestions. Did they feel the earth was better or worse without the human beings? The following is the development of the original Warau Indian myth about how people came to earth.

Once upon a time, before time began, human beings lived in the sky. Earth was empty of people. On earth, there were no people to:

<u>cut down trees</u>
<u>kill animals</u>
<u>pick flowers</u>
<u>pollute the rivers</u>.

It was very boring in the sky. In the sky they couldn't:

<u>make electricity</u>
<u>use mobile phones</u>
<u>drive cars</u>
<u>watch television</u>
<u>climb trees</u>
<u>swim in rivers</u>.

When they arrived on earth for the first time, they could:

<u>see</u> flowers, trees, butterflies, rivers,
<u>hear</u> birds singing, lions roaring, rivers rushing.

Example One day, a heavy hailstone fell through the sky and made a great hole down to earth. The people looked down the hole, and saw a wonderful land down below. Okonkwo was the first to climb down. Then all the others followed. Only one old lady got stuck in the hole and couldn't reach the earth. Instead, she remains until today in the sky and weeps, and weeps to be so far from her loved ones.

6.5 The Great Flood story: two red butterflies

Level Elementary and above

Time 20 minutes

Aims To work with adverbial phrases of time and place; to use vocabulary for animals, birds, and insects.

Procedure

1 Explain that you are going to tell an Inca creation myth, with the help of your class.

When you reach the underlined phrases, ask your class to share their own suggestions, using the same form: adverbial phrases of place in the first gap, lexical set of animals, birds, and insects in the second.

With a less advanced class you could practise before telling the story. Brainstorm with them prepositions used to describe places—*through, on, in, over, under, beyond, behind, up,* and *down*. Then, brainstorm with them animals they know.

There once was a boy who was walking in the mountains with his goat. One day, he heard a voice. It said, 'You must run to the highest mountain, because soon there will be a big, big flood. Take with you two of every animal, bird, and insect you meet on the way.' So he and the goat started their journey. They travelled

over the valleys
through the forest
through the Vale of Death
across the Deep Seas
across the Bogie River
through the caves of night

On the way, they met

two red butterflies
two lions
two big cats
two monkeys
two horses
two spiders, bees, wasps, ants
two snakes
two sheep
two cows
two pigs
two elephants

All of them walked in a long, long line. The line got

longer
and longer
and longer
and longer
and longer

and they all became more and more

tired
and hungry
and slow
and sleepy
and lazy
and worried

until at last they arrived at the highest mountain. They were all so happy that they gave a great roar. And just as they began to roar, the skies roared with them, and the rain began to fall, and fall, and fall, and fall, and fall.

The water rose higher, and higher, as all the animals, birds, insects, and the boy climbed higher, and higher, and higher, and higher.

At the top they all looked at the big wide world. It was covered in water.

2   Ask the learners to work in groups of two or three. Explain that there are some gaps in the story and that two people of every race on earth also joined them on top of the mountain. You may guide their discussion with questions. You could also encourage learners to use adverbial phrases of time and place in their sentences.

Examples   • How did the people arrive there?
   • How long did the animals, birds, insects, people of every race, and the boy wait on top of the mountain?
   • What happened next?

Variation

You could also ask the learners to take a sheet of blank paper. Each time you stop, and before you continue with the story, they should write as many ideas to continue it as they can in two minutes.

Comments

Your learners might be interested to know that this is the Machu Picchu myth, the story of the Inca city discovered at the top of a mountain in the Peruvian rainforest.

6.6 Learning from the guru: pictures in the sea

Level   **Pre-intermediate and above**

            The story can be adapted for elementary level

Time   **20 minutes**

Aim   **To practise the use of imperatives; to practise instructions and commands; to guess titles from text.**

Procedure

1   Read, or tell, your class the story extract below. Explain to them that the story is the answer to a question. Can they guess what the question is? What is the wise man trying to teach?

> First, close your eyes so your mind fills with deep dark sea.
>
> Then jump into the sea and let yourself swim.
>
> Swim deeper and deeper. Feel yourself floating.
>
> Float quietly so the sea is all round you, and also inside you.
>
> Let the sea wash in and out of your mind. Let it take you to strange places. You see pictures of people dead and alive, memories, dreams, places you knew as a child.
>
> At last, after eight hours in the deep dark sea, you see the sand again.
>
> Float quietly back to the sand. Roll gently onto the sand.
>
> Now open your eyes.

2   Invite learners' ideas about the question. Then explain to them that the request is: **teach me how to sleep.** The story comes from an African creation myth, where the land of the day and the land of the night were separate.

3   Ask your class to notice the language the wise man uses. What do all these verbs have in common?

Examples Jump   Swim   Roll
              Close   Feel   Open
              Let   Float

Explain that they are all commands or imperatives, and to form them we use the root of the verb.

You could prepare for the next stage by eliciting other commands that could be used by a teacher to a pupil.

Examples	Look	Notice	Think about
	Listen	Count	Remember
	Read		

4 Now tell your learners that they have also been invited to make a request. The request begins:

Teach me how to ...

Ask your learners to write their requests on a piece of paper. Below you will find some requests suggested by learners.

- Teach me how to be very clever.
- Teach me how to be rich.
- Teach me how to see the future.
- Teach me how to be patient and not get angry.

5 After two minutes, ask the learners to exchange their pieces of paper with a partner. Their task is to reply in writing to their partner's question, using imperative forms.

Follow-up

When the learners have written their instructions, they could be read aloud to the class without the request. The class could then guess the request.

6.7 Repetition story: the disappearing pot of gold

Level Elementary to pre-intermediate

Time 10 minutes

Aims To build teams and establish a 'storytelling' climate (this could be used as a warm-up or close-down activity); to repeat key structures with small changes of the subject slot and adverbs of place; to listen for connections.

Procedure

1 If you can, have your class sit in a circle. Tell them you are about to tell a story, but you can't finish it without their help. If they listen hard, they will know how to do this. Start this story.

A man one day found a pot of gold. 'I must hide it, otherwise someone will steal it from me,' he thought. So he hid the pot of gold *under a tree*. He hid it so well that he forgot where it was. Then one day, *an old lady* was sitting under the tree and saw the pot of gold. 'I must hide it, otherwise someone will steal it from me,' she thought. So she hid the pot of gold in a cave. She hid it so well that she forgot where it was. Then one day, a ...

2   When you reach this point, ask the learners to suggest how they think the story should go on. This will be a repetition, and the story can continue indefinitely, with new people finding the pot of gold and hiding it in a different place. Let the story grow organically, with each learner having a chance to repeat the chant, or take it somewhere new. If your learners are at elementary level, you may want to write the sentence frame on the board to make the repetition simpler.

Example

> Then one day, a/an ... found the pot of gold ... in/on/under ... (previous place).
>   'I must hide it, otherwise someone will steal it from me,' he/she thought. So she/he hid the pot of gold ... (new place). He/she hid it so well that he/she forgot where it was.

3   Let the story come to a natural end, when everyone has had a turn. An 'open' ending with no real conclusion could itself be part of the story.

Follow-up

If you wish to take this storytelling activity into a written phase, ask the learners to write up their own version for homework. A less advanced class could use the structure at step 2 as a framework to write the story. More advanced classes could develop the story in their own way.

Variation

You could also use names of learners to continue the story, and bring each learner in to finish a sentence.

Then one day, Faizal was ...

Then, Faizal brings in the next learner by naming him/her, and so on around the class.

7

Voices in stories

Stories don't need to be a simple narrative told through the voice of a single narrator. A writer can invent and become a hundred different voices. The writer can be the highly personal voice of the main character, recording inner thoughts through diaries and intense love letters, or he/she can look at the main characters coldly from the outside as a psychologist writing a report about a distraught lover, a journalist writing an article, or a travel brochure writing an assessment of the character's home town. In this way we can look at characters from different angles. Not just what they do or what they think, but what others see and think about them, too. This chapter will look at how to build stories using different kinds of texts. We can tell a story using different text types, so that it is not just one simple and linear narration. To do so, we can use a portfolio of voices to tell the story from several angles and in several different ways, just as a biographer builds up the story of his/her subject.

In this chapter we shall use one story, *The love potion*, as an example. This is a story in which the lover wins his beloved by drinking what he believes to be a magic potion. The activities show how this story can be built up using different elements:

- letters from the lover declaring his love (activity 7.1)
- letters from the beloved rejecting him (activity 7.1)
- doctor's report describing the symptoms of lovesickness (activity 7.2)
- advertising leaflets for the love potion (activity 7.3)
- a lover's diary describing the effects of the love potion (activity 7.4)
- the beloved's diary describing her changing feelings (activity 7.4)
- a newspaper announcement of the lovers' surprise engagement (activity 7.5)
- a radio commentary on the village wedding (activity 7.6).

The teacher can divide up any story of their choice into a 'portfolio' of different text types and different voices. These can be used in many interesting ways:

- to practise the features of different text types
- as a 'dossier' for reading practice with other classes. Classes can then reconstruct the story using the information they have.
- to create a 'theatre script' by reading the different text types aloud, with personal voices contrasted with public voices, inner voices with outer voices: What do people *say*? What do people *write*? What do people *think*? What do others think about *them*? Read aloud, this makes for an exciting story.

Material

The following story is used for all of the activities in this chapter.

Nemorino was terribly in love with Adina, a beautiful and clever girl in his village. She laughed at him, and told him there was no hope. She could never love him, because she had too many things to do in life. She had no time for love. But he was dying for love and did not know what to do. Then, one day, a travelling doctor came to town, and the young man explained his problem.

'No problem, you can buy a bottle of my love potion!' said the doctor. 'It will make you so loveable that no woman could resist you!'

Eagerly, Nemorino bought the bottle, using every penny he had. He drank the bottle right down to the bottom.

At the same time, without his knowledge, his old sick uncle had died and had left him all his fortune. He was now rich! All the girls in the village, except Adina, knew the news. Just as Nemorino finished the bottle, they arrived, in their brightest skirts, with their hair in ribbons and baskets of flowers to perfume them. They all danced around him, laughing and throwing flowers at him and trying to win his attention.

Just then, Adina walked past.

'Oh, he has forgotten me already!' she thought. 'As soon as I reject him, he goes and flirts with other girls!'

First she was angry, then jealous, then hurt, then angry with herself.

'Maybe I was wrong after all to reject him. After all, he looks so handsome and loveable, and look how the girls love him! And of all the girls, it was *me* he really wanted.' She felt very sorry indeed. Then the doctor walked by.

'I can sell you some of my love potion!' he said. 'Look how well it worked for Nemorino!'

'Certainly not!' she retorted. '*I* don't need a love potion. I have my *own* charms to win him.'

She did indeed. She walked past Nemorino with her dazzling smile, then looked away proudly.

'The love potion has worked!' he thought.

Of course, he was right.

This is the plot of Donizetti's opera, *L'elisir d'amore*.

7.1 Letters lovely and not so lovely

Some wonderful stories have been written as a series of letters between the characters. The first one written in this way in English was *Clarissa*, by Samuel Richardson. Letters can tell the whole story, or be part of the story in order to allow characters to speak for themselves, and show us what they are really thinking.

Level Intermediate and above

Time 20–40 minutes

Aims To write a letter.

Preparation

Write a letter opening on the board.

Example Dear ... ,
I have wanted to tell you this for a long time, but I have been too shy. I cannot live without you any longer.

Procedure

1 Ask your learners to read the letter on the blackboard. Open a discussion about the letter, using the questions below as examples.
   - *Is the person writing young or old, male or female?*
   - *Is the receiver of the letter young or old, male or female?*
   - *What do you think is the situation?*
   - *What do you think the reply will be?*

2 Ask each learner to choose the answers they liked best in the discussion, and make a short note of them. You may help them by writing the key words on the board.

Example *Writer:*   male/female, young/old
Receiver: male/female, young/old
Situation: (one sentence)

Suggestion from students

WRITER: an old man who runs a cafe. He has worked there for a long time.

RECEIVER: she sits in the cafe every day and works on the book that she's writing. She is very poor, but the book will make her rich.

SITUATION: the old man watches her every day. He wants to know what she is writing. But she never looks at him. Soon she will be very famous and very rich. She won't go to that cafe any more but to a big restaurant.

3 Now, ask your class to work in groups of two or three. Ask them to share with the group the characters and situations they have described, and choose the one they like best.

4 Ask each learner to write the first letter to the beloved. Make sure your class knows how a letter should be laid out.

5 After ten minutes, ask the learners to sign their letter, using a fictional name of their choice. Then, they should exchange their letters with a partner.

6 The partners should now reply to the letter they have received. This could be done for homework. At the beginning of the next lesson, the learners could share the answers to the letters with the class.

Variation 1

Tell your learners the story at the opening of this chapter. Then ask them to:

a write Nemorino's letter to Adina at the beginning and at the end of the story.

b write Adina's letter to Nemorino at the beginning and at the end of the story.

Variation 2

Here are other letter openings you could use. You can choose those that suit your learners' level, and then follow the same steps as in activity 7.1.

Example 1 Dear … ,
I am writing to tell you I can never love you.

Example 2 Dear … ,
This is something I have never told anyone. I am writing to you, because I think you will understand.

Example 3 Dear … ,
I am writing to tell you I am about to leave on a long journey. I don't know when I will return, or when you will see me again. Before I leave, I want to explain my reasons.

Comments

In the case of Variation 2, example 1: this letter is likely to use present simple verbs describing current feelings.

In the case of Variation 2, example 2: this letter is likely to use past simple to describe events or feelings in the past.

In the case of Variation 2, example 3: this letter is likely to use structures that refer to the future, and to future hopes and aspirations. This may include modals for speculation, such as: *I may, I might, I would like to.*

7.2 Doctors' reports: advice for the lovesick

Level Pre-intermediate and above

Time 20 minutes

Aims To use nouns connected with *-sick* and *-ache*, and their meaning in different compounds; to describe physical symptoms; to give advice; to take notes from short interviews.

Procedure

1 Write the words and phrases below on the board.

A	B
lovesick	sick
homesick	
heartbroken	broken leg
heartache	headache

Ask the learners to tell you how the words in column A are different from the words in column B.

Example They are about feelings.
They are in the mind.
No doctor can mend them. Only life can mend them.
There is no medicine for these feelings.

2 Explain to the learners they are going to write doctor's notes to help the sick patient in column A. To do this, they must prepare the doctor's questions. Elicit from the class three or four 'doctor's questions' and write them on the board. With a less advanced class, you may want to explain the word 'symptoms'.

Examples What is your problem?
What are your symptoms?
How long have you felt this way?
How often do you feel like this?
When does it feel bad?

3 Ask the learners to work in groups of three.
PARTNER A: you're the doctor. Ask the questions suggested on the board.
PARTNER B: you're the patient. Decide on your problem and your situation. Give your character a name.
PARTNER C: write notes on the conversation, using key words.

Example

Name:	Nemorino
Problem:	lovesick
Symptoms:	heart beats very fast, red face, wet hands, not able to speak, forgetful, awake all night, can't concentrate, can't work
How long:	six months
How often:	every day, 485 times a day
When:	whenever he sees Adina, whenever he does not see Adina

4 When the group have finished their interview, ask them to decide together on a cure. Suggest the following verb forms to give advice:
- commands: *make, do, take*
- modals: *You should/ought to/must*

Example

> ## Cure for patient
>
> Drink a love potion
>
> Make Adina jealous
>
> Have a haircut
>
> Wear perfume
>
> Invite her to a wonderful dinner

Variation

Read the story at the start of this chapter to the class. Ask them to imagine that Nemorino is at the doctor's. Prepare doctor's notes for Nemorino's condition.

7.3 Advertisements: magical medicines

Level Intermediate and above

Time 30 minutes

Aims To use adjectives to describe positive qualities; to use *It can* ... to describe abilities; to work with superlatives and comparatives; to learn about some features of advertisement: key information in an advertisement.

Preparation

Copy the box below onto the board.

> ## Magical medicines
>
> a a medicine to make you loveable
>
> b a medicine to make you very clever
>
> c a medicine to make you very beautiful

Procedure

1 Invite the learners to suggest other medicines they would like included in the list and add them to the list on the board.

2 Explain that the class needs to write an advertisement/publicity leaflet to try and sell these medicines. Elicit some ideas about what should be included in the advertisement.

- What does the medicine do?
- Why is it better than all other medicines?
- Provide some quotations from happy customers.
- How is the medicine made?
- The ingredients of the medicine.
- Before and after using the medicine: photos and stories.

With less advanced groups, you can focus on the first two questions in the list, and practise:

- Modals to describe abilities: It *can* ... (make you happy/ intelligent/ clever/ loveable)
- Superlatives: It is *the most/the best/the ... -est* medicine (*the most useful, the most popular, the cheapest*)

3   When at least five ideas are on the board, ask the learners to work in groups of three or four. Each group should choose one medicine from the list, or a medicine of their own choice. Their task is now to write an advertisement by answering the questions on the board.

4   After 15 minutes, ask groups to share their advertisements with the class. They could be read aloud or posted around the room.

5   Ask the class to choose just one medicine they would like to buy. Ask for a show of hands. The medicine with the most votes is the 'winner'.

Variations

Read the story at the start of this chapter. Ask the learners to write an advertisement for Nemorino's love potion.

Follow-up

As a follow-up, ask the learners to imagine the effects of the medicine they have chosen on a story character of their choice.

Example
- What happens next?
- How does he/she feel?

7.4 Diaries

Level   **Elementary and above**

Time   **30 minutes**

Aims   **To learn to write a first person narrative; to learn about a diary/journal features; to look at a story from several points of view; to learn about different formats for writing dates.**

Procedure

1   Tell the learners the story at the start of this chapter.

2   Ask the learners some questions about the story.

Examples   How many characters are there in the story?

Who are they? (Nemorino, Adina, the doctor, the girls in the village)

3 Ask the class to choose a specific period of time when the story takes place. Write the dates on the board.

Example Date when Nemorino first meets Adina: 1st June 2004.

Date when they finally get married: 1st June 2005.

4 Now divide the class into four groups. Give each group one character from the story. Ask them to think of three dates between the beginning and the end of the story that correspond to different events.

5 Their task is to answer the questions below for a diary entry for each of the dates they have chosen. Write the questions on the board for the students to have as a guide. The questions for the diary entries can be adapted to meet the level of the class. The examples here are for elementary-level learners.

Example **21st June 2004**

- *Who did you see?* I saw the doctor today.
- *What did you say?* I said, 'Please help me! I love Adina!'
- *What did you do?* I bought a bottle of love medicine.
- *How did you feel?* I felt so happy.

Depending on the level of your learners, you can practise adjectives for feelings (*happy, sad, shy, worried, lonely, lovesick, angry*) before starting the activity.

6 Once all groups have answered the questions, ask them to write the diary entry in note form.

Example **1st June 2004**

- Met a boy called Nemorino today.
- He's really shy. He goes red when he talks.
- Perhaps sick? Don't know!
- I pretended I didn't see him.

7 When each group has written their three diary entries for their characters, ask them to read back their entries in chronological order. This will generate an interesting piece of 'three-way' narrative.

Example 1st June: Adina's diary entry.
21st June: Nemorino's diary entry.
24th June: doctor's diary entry.

Variation 1

You can use any other story in this book for this activity, following the same procedures.

Variation 2

Once your learners have understood the idea of using a diary to establish multiple viewpoints, encourage them to return to stories they have already written in other activities, and write diary entries for their characters.

7.5 Newspaper articles

Level   Intermediate and above

Time   30 minutes

Aims   To write and interpret newspaper headlines; to find out information in a newspaper article; to match content and headline/title.

Procedure

1   Tell the story at the start of this chapter, or any story you would like to share with your class. Ask your learners: if you were a newspaper journalist, which part of the story would you write about?

Examples   The doctor exposed as a hoax/fraud/sham/fake.
The announcement of the uncle's death and Nemorino's new wealth.
The engagement of Nemorino and Adina.

2   Give the learners a few minutes to write a newspaper headline for their news stories.

Example   Fake doctor pretends to mend hearts!
Local boy becomes a millionaire!
Surprise love match announced!

3   Ask the learners to share their headlines with the class. Compare the different headlines for each story, and ask the learners to vote for the one they like best.

4   Brainstorm with the learners the information they would need to put into each story. Write their suggestions on the board. Here is a possible guide.

Example   **Information in newspaper stories**
   - Interview with the main characters in the story
   - Two or three key facts
   - What one or two people have said about the main character/s (best friends, family, observers, experts)
   - An opinion about the main character.

5   For homework, or in class, ask the learners now to choose one newspaper story and use the information list above to prepare it. A group of three or four learners could divide up the work, taking one aspect of the story each.

Follow-up

Ask each group of learners to give in their stories and write their headline on the board. Shuffle the stories and give each group a new one. Their task is to read the story, and match it with the correct headline on the board.

7.6 Radio commentaries

Level Pre-intermediate and above

Time 30 minutes

Aims To practise the use of present continuous in commentaries of current action; to describe current actions; to practise the language of spoken commentaries.

Preparation

Select a story you would like to discuss with the class. Below you have some possibilities. Choose the event you think would be the most exciting for your learners and get ready to retell the story in the chosen style and point of view.

Examples *Red Riding Hood*: the arrest of the wolf—nature commentary about the behaviour of wolves.

The love-potion story: the village wedding of Nemorino and Adina (see the beginning of this chapter).

The love-potion story: medical programme on the effects of the love potion.

The Pied Piper story: the rats being piped out of the village (see Chapter 9).

The jungle creature: nature commentary about the animal in the jungle (see activity 10.8).

Procedure

1 Ask your learners what they think is the difference between a newspaper article and a commentary on the radio. Elicit that, while one describes an event that is finished/in the past, the other describes an event as it happens. The speaker doesn't know what is going to happen next. The verb form used is the present continuous.

2 Explain to your learners that you are a news commentator, and you are present at one of the key events in the chosen story.

3 Read to your learners the passage you have prepared from your chosen story. Below you will find some examples from the stories suggested above. Ask them to guess which story you are retelling.

Example 1 Now, yes, I can see, just appearing from behind the trees ... Oh dear me! It looks like a very curious wolf. Mmm ..., I think, yes, it seems to be following the little girl ... very quietly, we shouldn't disturb it ... Now, let's see what it's doing now, ... (*Red Riding Hood*).

Example 2 Now we're all gathered here in the village to see what this rat-catcher with the pipe will do. Great excitement here! Yes, you can feel the excitement here, waiting for him to arrive. Oh yes! ... Here he is ... quite a character ... getting ready to start the magic. What will that be? We're all waiting. None of us quite know ... (*Pied Piper*).

4 Ask the learners to notice the language of your examples.

Examples   *exclamations:* Oh yes!
noises to show response to events: Mmm …
utterances rather than complete sentences: Great excitement here!
pauses while things happen: …

5 When you have established the idea of 'radio commentary', ask your learners to choose an event in their own story/in *The love potion story*/in a story of their choice, and write 30 seconds of radio commentary (about 250 words).

6 After ten minutes, ask the learners to read their commentaries to a partner, for them to answer questions on it.

Examples   • Which story is being described?
• Which event is being described?
• What is going to happen next?

Acknowledgements

I am indebted to my colleague Rob Pope, and Oxford Brookes student Sally Anne Thomas, for the idea of a 'nature commentary' about Red Riding Hood's wolf. The version here is based on Sally Anne's piece, for which we awarded an A+.

8

Story games

These activities can be used as five-minute warm-ups or closures at the beginning or end of the class. They involve the learners in guessing, playing, interacting, and in mini-competitions. Some lead to group stories developed by the whole class. Others allow a 'silent' period for learners to listen to you telling a story, but require listening skills such as prediction, completion, interpretation, and formulating a standpoint. These game-like and group ways of telling stories help a class to gel, and individuals to develop confidence. These activities also encourage learners to share jokes and puzzles in their mother tongue, so they can be used with elementary up to advanced learners.

8.1 Joke exchange

Level **Elementary and above**

Time **20 minutes**

Aim **To develop story comprehension through the understanding of main ideas; to predict the final line of a story; to understand punch lines.**

Procedure

1 Tell the learners the joke below. You could change the underlined words in the story by adding local foods and the local currency to replace the ones here.

Invite them to suggest the punch line, the final line of the story. The 'real' punch line is:
'You see!', the rich friend said, 'they're working already!'

2 Ask your learners to work in groups of two or three and think about jokes they have enjoyed at home with family or friends. Give groups ten minutes to exchange jokes with one another. With elementary learners, the jokes could be told in their mother tongue.

> Two friends were sitting side by side on the bus. One of them was very rich and successful. Everything he did turned to gold. The other was very miserable. None of his jobs worked out and he was always losing money. After a while, the poor friend said to the rich one: 'What makes you so clever?' The rich friend thought for a while. '*Shrimps*,' he said at last. They both sat there, considering this. Then the rich friend took a plastic lunch box out of his bag and opened it. Inside were *shrimps, cooked in oil and spices*. He began eating, one by one, with his fingers. The poor friend watched, miserably. Then he said, 'How much to buy your shrimps?' '100 *ringgit*,' the other one said. The poor friend dug in his pockets and pulled out all the change he could find until he could pay. 'Here,' he said. 'Hand them over. I'll buy them.' As the bus jogged along, he began eating the shrimps, one by one. After a while, he said, 'Hey! That's very expensive for a box of shrimps! They only cost 12 ringgit in the market.'

3   Ask each group to choose the joke they liked best, and tell it to the rest of the class. If the joke has a punch line ask them to save it and invite the class to suggest it. Elementary groups could tell the joke in their mother tongue, with only the punch line being translated into English.

Variation 1

Another interesting variation is as follows. Ask the learners to think about jokes they know.

They should, then, write down the punch line on a piece of paper, and hand it to a partner.

The task of the partner is to guess the joke by working backwards from the punch line.

When every learner has invented a joke, they could share these in groups of five or six.

The joke that elicits most laughter is the winner.

8.2 Puzzle stories: the wise man and the fool

Level   Elementary and above
        The story can be adapted for elementary learners.
Time   **20 minutes**
Aims   **To learn to interpret a text; to work at solving problems.**

Procedure
1   Tell your class the story below.

> In the village, there was a very wise man and a very foolish man. They happened to look so similar that it was sometimes impossible to tell the difference. One day, a villager found the wise/foolish man in the street. He was bent over, so no one could see who he was. 'What are you doing?' she asked. 'I'm looking for my keys. I can't get into my shop without them.' More and more people joined in, crawling up and down the street on their hands and knees, looking under stones, and under dustbins, and on doorsteps. At last, someone asked, 'Where did you last see your keys?' 'In my house,' said the wise/foolish man. 'Then why are you looking for your keys here in the street?' 'Because there's more light here!' he said.
>
> Was it the wise man or the foolish man?

2 After you have told the story to your class, ask them to think about the question at the end. Have a show of hands to find out the answer to these other questions.

Example
- How many thought it was the wise man?
- How many thought it was the foolish man?
- Can they explain why?

3 Ask the learners to develop a story of their own with the title:

Silly or clever? Which is it?

They can base their story on:

- real experiences of their own
- experiences overheard or read about
- stories and jokes in their own language
- an idea of their own.

For less advanced learners, the following framework can be used:

> In the ... there was a very wise man and a very foolish man. They happened to look so similar that it was sometimes impossible to tell the difference. One day, ...
>
> The villagers said, '...?'
>
> The man said, '...'
>
> Was he the wise man or the fool?

Example In the city there was a very wise man and a very foolish man. They happened to look so similar that it was sometimes impossible to tell the difference. One day, the people saw one of the men going down the street. He was pulling a bag of money behind him on a chain.

'Why are you doing that?' the people said.

'So it won't run away!' the man said.

Was he the wise man or the fool?

8.3 Story dominoes

Level   Intermediate and above

Time   10 minutes

Aims   To recognize and use repetition as a cohesive device; to work with connections between sentences.

Procedure

1   If you have a small class, place your learners in a circle. If you have a big group, learners could work in rows from where they are sitting.

2   This is a game that explores connections and cohesion between sentences. Explain you are going to start a class story. Each person in the class is going to add a sentence to it. The learners must start their sentence with the last two or three words of the sentence before. If a person is unable to continue the story, they can stop, and start a new story. The winners are the learners who can keep the story going for the most sentences.

3   Start the story with a line from any of the stories in this book, or from the story openings in activity 2.1.

The clock struck thirteen when it happened

It happened so suddenly that nobody could stop it.

'Stop it!' she shouted, as the thief ran out of the door with the priceless painting.

The priceless painting was of her father, the king.

The king would be furious if he found out.

---

4   You might want to record the story in some way, so you can report back to the class at a later stage about how they have connected sentences.

Variation 1

This game can also be played in written form, with learners writing their sentences on a piece of paper, and passing it to their neighbour. The neighbour adds a sentence, and so on until the end of the story or until every learner has had a turn to write. The final story can then be read aloud.

Variation 2

The game can also be played with each person giving two or three sentences. It is a little easier to build a story this way.

8.4 Story consequences

Level Elementary and above

Time 10 minutes

The game could be played two or three times in a lesson.

Aims To develop listening skills through story dictation; to identify stages in a story; to work at sentence completion.

Procedure

1 Ask the learners to sit either in a circle, or in groups of ten around the room. Each learner needs to have a blank piece of paper. Tell them you are going to read to them ten sentence beginnings and they will have to write down the complete sentence on their sheet of paper. Then they will have to fold the paper over so the sentence is hidden and pass it on to their neighbour on the right. This procedure will be repeated for each sentence you read out.

Example There once was a ____ who lived in a ____
He/she was very happy, but he/she had one problem: ____.
One day, he/she met a ____ on the way to ____
He said, ____
She said, ____
Then she ____
So they decided to solve the problem together. What they did was ____
Next they ____
Then they ____
At last, the problem was solved.

2 When you have finished reading out all ten sentences, ask each learner to unfold their piece of paper. Ask them to work in groups of four or five, and read out their complete stories to one another.

3 Ask each group to choose their favourite story to read out to the whole class.

Follow-up

As a follow-up, ask the learners to take their story home and edit it, using one of the editing checklists in Chapter 10. These focus on editing for accuracy, vocabulary, ideas, variety, cohesion, punctuation, and characterization. Select one of these depending on the focus you wish for your lesson.

Variations

You can include in the list of sentences any aspect of story that you wish to develop.

For example, the five senses: He/She could *see/smell/hear* ...

Indirect speech: *she said that* ... | *he said that* ...

8.5 Sequencing race

Level Elementary and above

Time 10 minutes

Aims To identify cohesive links in a story; to use cohesive clues to find the sequence in a story.

Preparation

Choose a story your learners do not know. Take the main events of the story and write each event on a label. You will need one set of labels that tells the complete story for each group.

The town was full of rats.	The head of the town council invited the famous rat-catcher to town.
He arrived carrying only a pipe.	He played the pipe and all the rats followed him.
A month later he returned and asked for money for his work.	The head of the town council said, 'What? All you did was play your pipe!'
So the rat-catcher played his pipe again. This time all the children ran out of their houses.	He led them out of the town, and they all disappeared over the hill never to be seen again.

Procedure

1 Divide your class into groups of three or four. Give each group a set of story labels. Explain that the labels tell a story. The task of each group is to put the labels in a sequence that is cohesive and tells a good story. The first group to do this is the winner.

2 Ask the winners to tell the story according to the sequence they have chosen, using their own words. Ask the class to judge whether the story is cohesive and coherent—that is, whether they think it is a good story and makes sense.

Variation 1

Divide the class in groups of four, and ask each group to think of a story. They could prepare their own set of 'events' labels by dividing up a blank sheet of A4 into eight and writing on each rectangle the main events. Circulate to make sure the learners are writing correct and clear sentences on each label. Each label needs to include one of the main events written as a simple statement. They can now play the game, with each group using the stories of a different one. Ensure learners do not work with their own stories.

Variation 2

A good variation for elementary-level learners is to play the game using pictures instead of words. Once the sequence has been found, learners could label each one with a short sentence or key words.

Variation 3

A more advanced group may enjoy the following variation. Choose *two* stories your learners do not know. Prepare a set of 'event' labels for the two stories for each group. Hand out a set to each group. They must now work out which events belong to which story. This is an excellent team problem-solving activity, and involves detailed reading skills.

8.6 Story bluff

Level   Intermediate and above

Time   30 minutes

Aims   To practise writing story summaries; to predict content from a story title.

Preparation

1   Select a story you have read or heard—and which your learners do not know—for each group. You could use the stories in this book.

2   Prepare a label listing the story title and a short summary of the story for each group.

Nemorino and the love potion

Nemorino was in love with Adina, but she did not love him.

One day, Nemorino bought a magic medicine from the doctor. The doctor promised that when Nemorino drank the medicine every woman would fall in love with him.

The same day, Nemorino's uncle died and left all his money to him. Nemorino was rich.

Suddenly all the girls wanted to marry him.

Adina became very jealous. Then she realized he was very handsome.

Then she fell in love with him.

The love potion had worked.

Procedure

1 Divide the class into groups of three or four. Explain to your learners that each group is going to get a story title and its summary. Their task will be to plan three more 'false summaries' that match the title. This can be done orally, with learners writing notes as a memory aid. The aim is to make the other summaries so convincing that it is difficult to choose which the 'correct' one is.

2 Each group should then be given a turn to play the game. They should give the class the title of their story. Then they will tell the class the four summaries: the 'correct' one, and the three invented by them. The class must guess which the correct one is. The team that guesses the most correct summaries is the winner.

8.7 The shrinking saga

Level Intermediate and above

Time 10 minutes

The game can be played two or three times in the lesson.

Aims To work at editing a story down to its minimum possible length; to work at reducing sentences whilst keeping them grammatically correct.

Preparation

You will need to prepare a 'mini-story' so each learner can read and work with it. You can either write it on the board or provide copies for learners. Below is one example. Another suitable story is *Tomaso's magic hut* in activity 1.6.

Example When the old man died, he left his little hut to his son. The son worked hard, sold the hut, and built a house. When he died, he left the house to his daughter. The daughter worked hard, sold the house, and built a beautiful castle. When the daughter died, she left the castle to her son. The son worked hard, sold the castle, and went to live in a little hut. He liked small places much better than big, cold castles. (82 words)

Procedure

1 Write the word *mini-saga* on the board. Explain that they are stories on humorous, bizarre, or autobiographical themes with very strict rules. If necessary, write these rules on the board.

A mini-saga must be exactly 50 words in length.

A mini-saga should contain the key ingredients of story: character, situation, and plot. (See activity 1.1 for story ingredients.)

The title must not contain more than 15 words.

Hyphenated words count as two words.

Contractions such as *won't* or *can't* count as one word.

2 Divide the class into teams of three or four. Give each team a copy of the mini-story you have chosen. Their task is to reduce it to a mini-saga of fifty words. Remind the learners that the sentences need to be grammatically correct, and the story needs to be clear and coherent. Give them ten minutes to do this, and time them.

3 After ten minutes, stop the class. Ask each team to read back their mini-sagas.

Ask the class to vote on the best one. (Learners are not allowed to vote for their own team!)

Variation

This game can also be played as story expansion. Give the learners just one sentence of a story, and ask them to 'build' the story into fifty words. The winning mini-saga is the one that is grammatically accurate and reads as a coherent story with the key story ingredients of character, situation, and plot.

Follow-up

As a follow-up, ask the learners to write their own 50-word mini-saga. Give them 15 minutes to do this. At the end, ask them to 'correct' one another's stories. Ask them to follow the criteria discussed for the mini-sagas.

Below is an example of a mini-saga based on a teacher's childhood memories:

There was a boy who was naughty at school. The only subject he was good at was painting. So the teacher asked him to paint the scenery for the school play. He painted the scenery, but, unfortunately, he also painted spectacles and a moustache on the portrait of the headmaster.

8.8 Story mime

Level Elementary and above

Time 30 minutes

Aims To convert pictures to narrative; to convert actions to narrative; to integrate listening and writing skills; to summarize a story; to edit summaries.

Preparation

Photocopy the picture stories below, so that each group has one. It does not matter how large the group is, because they will need to change the story to match the number of learners in the group. Each group needs to have a different story.

Picture Story 1

Photocopiable © Oxford University Press

Picture Story 3   See the 'City Monkeys' story, 2.6 (page 37).

Story 4   See the 'Repetition Story', 6.7 (page 95)

Procedure

1 Divide the learners into four groups. Give each group one of the picture stories. Each story outline can be acted out with any number of characters.

2 Explain to the learners they are going to 'tell' the story without using any words. Ask them to plan and rehearse their story, so every learner in the group has a part. This may mean adding or subtracting characters in the story.

3 After ten minutes 'rehearsal' time, ask each group to act out their story.

4 Once the story is over, ask each group to make a summary of what they have seen. They have five minutes to do this.

5 After five minutes, ask each group to present their summary. The group that acted out the story should choose the best summary. Below you will find the criteria that should be proposed to learners. You, as teacher, could also choose the summary that is the most coherent and accurate.

The story includes all the main events and all the main characters that appeared in the original story.

Variation

Learners could prepare mime stories of their own, then follow the same procedures as above for the miming and summary writing stages.

Acknowledgements

I am grateful to Tom Hunter and Jenny Pearson for introducing me to the first two mime stories, and to the Swedish teachers in Oxford for acting them out so well.

9
Performing story

Any of the story activities in this book can lead to either a written story, or a story read, performed, or told aloud. The oral storytelling tradition is universal, and includes the recounting of whole sagas in temples, the telling of personal anecdotes about a loved one at weddings and funerals, story as performance, such as pantomime, puppet shows, classroom sketches, community theatre, and the telling of nursery tales at bedtime to a child. Some of these are communal and public; others are about quiet and personal moments between friends and family members. Yet all can be enhanced by some of the techniques suggested below.

The activities in this chapter will draw on the story below as an example. However, the activities will work equally well with any story you choose.

> In the city were thousands of rats. Rats everywhere. Rats in the houses, rats in the rivers, rats up the chimneys, rats in the soup, rats in the cupboards, rats in the beds, rats in the street, and rats in the schools. The town council had a big meeting. They decided to ask the famous rat-catcher to come to the city and lead the rats away. The next day he arrived, with a long pipe. 'A pipe?' they said. 'We expected poison, or traps, or pieces of cheese, but all he's brought with him is a pipe!' He stood in the High Street and blew his pipe. It made a long, long whistle. Then all the rats appeared, from houses, and rivers, chimneys and soup bowls, cupboards, baths and beds, streets and schools, they all came running. The man with the pipe walked down the High Street, over the hill, and out of the city, and all the rats went running after him. The next day the rat-catcher went to the head of the town council. 'Pay me for my services,' he said. 'Pay you?! All you brought with you was a pipe—no cheese, or poison, or traps, or cages. Go back to where you came from!' 'I will indeed,' said the rat-catcher. He stood in the High Street and played his pipe again. This time, there came running from the schools, and streets, and rivers and forests, and beds and baths and bowls of soup, all the children of the city. And they followed him, down the street, over the hill, and out of the city, laughing and playing and singing and chattering. Just one little boy, with a broken leg, was left behind. He sat at the end of the street, and watched his best friend disappear behind the hill, never to be seen again.

9.1 Memorizing stories

Level Intermediate and above

Time 30 minutes

Aims To practise techniques for memorizing stories; to develop confidence in telling stories aloud from memory.

Preparation

1 Make copies of two mini-stories, so that each student has a story to read. You can use the mini-story at the beginning of this chapter, and one of your own or one from this book.

2 The students will also need blank sheets of paper, scissors, and coloured pens.

3 Make copies of the following Memory Worksheet so each student has a copy.

Memory worksheet: techniques for memorizing stories

- Read the story two or three times. Then note down what you remember of the main events, using key words only.
- Make five or six small labels from a blank sheet of paper. Write on each label one or two key words to remind you of the sequence of events in the story. You can hold the labels in the palm of your hand and use them to guide you through the story.
- Draw the events of the story on a blank sheet of paper.
- Draw a chart, spidergram, or 'bubble chart' with the main events and characters in the story. Write the events or names in different colours on your bubble chart or notes, as a memory trigger.
- Plan a visual 'prop' for each stage of the story: for example, a whistle for the Pied Piper, a rolled-up decree for the head of the town council, a stick for the little boy with the broken leg. Either draw these props or write them down as key words on your label, or actually create these props from objects in the classroom.

Procedure

1 Tell your learners you are going to practise memorizing and telling stories by heart. Ask them:

- *Why do you think it's a good idea to remember stories by heart?*
- *What's good about it? What's bad about it?*

You can use some of the ideas below to help the discussion. Write their ideas on the blackboard as a reference throughout this lesson.

Advantages of memorizing a story

You can improvise, adding your own words and phrases.

It is easier to respond to the audience. For example, if they like the repetitive parts, you can make them longer, add more phrases, invite the audience to join in with their own suggestions.

You can keep eye contact with the class all the way through.

You can move about the room, use your arms and hands, and 'act' more if you do not have a book in your hands.

Special warning: do not try to memorize the actual words of the story. There are dangers in doing this. For example, you might forget the words and lose your direction, even though you know the events of the story well. Instead, memorize the characters, your knowledge of what they do and say, and the events themselves, so that every time you tell the story it will be a natural 'retelling'.

2   Now hand out the memory worksheet. With your class, discuss ways you could use each technique with a story familiar to them. Use the blackboard to record key words and ideas, and to improvise drawings and charts. Below are some examples of memory techniques for stories in this book:

3   Divide the students into pairs. Give partner A the first story, and partner B the second story. Explain they have ten minutes to read the story and that they should use any technique they find helpful to remember the story.

4   After ten minutes, ask the students to exchange the story texts. Each student should now tell their story from memory; the partner should check with the text, to make sure the main events and characters are included.

5   Ask the students to nominate the partners who told the best stories. Nominate two students to tell their stories to the whole class.

6   Use the 'Advantages of memorizing a story' checklist on the blackboard, to identify with your class the good things about each student's performance.

Homework

Ask the students to memorize another story of their choice to share with the class, perhaps the story of a book or film they have read or seen recently.

They can use any memory technique that helps them and can prepare drawings, objects, and labels to bring to the lesson.

Example 1 Spidergram

Example 2 Bubble chart

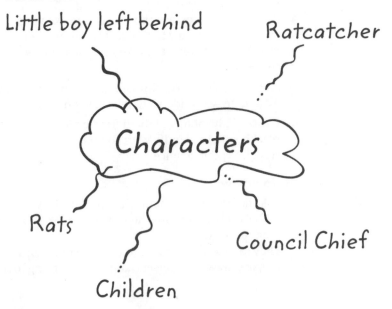

Council meeting

Arrival of the ratcatcher

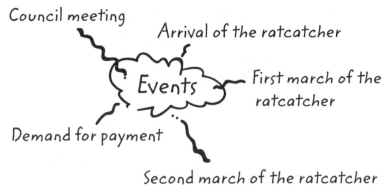

Events

First march of the ratcatcher

Demand for payment

Second march of the ratcatcher

The council chamber

Settings

Streets in the town

9.2 Reading stories aloud

Level   Pre-intermediate and above

Time   30 minutes

Aims   To practise techniques for reading stories aloud.

Preparation

Copy two stories so that each student has a copy of one story to read aloud.

Copy the checklist below, so each student has a copy.

Checklist for reading aloud

Look at your audience often.

Speak out towards your audience, and not down to the paper.

Do not speak too fast. You can see the paper, but your audience can't!

Pause at the end of paragraphs.

Change your voice to show feelings in the story: surprise, anger, fear, and so on.

Change your voice to show the different characters in the story.

Procedure

1   Tell the students you are going to practise reading stories aloud from a text.

Ask them:

- *What is good about reading stories aloud from the text?*
- *What are the problems of reading stories aloud from the text?*
- *What do you like best about listening to stories?*
- *What do you like best about telling stories?*

Below are some ideas that might help the discussion. Write learners' ideas on the board as a reference through this activity.

Reading a story aloud

Reading a story aloud is helpful if you are not quite sure what is going to happen in the story, or if it is a longer, more complicated story.

It is enjoyable if the writing is particularly beautiful and effective.

It is useful if students have, or will have, copies of the text themselves for comparison and more detailed study.

The book itself can be one of your 'props', which you could pass round, hold up, or simply use to establish a 'book culture' in your classroom.

2   Now give each student a copy of the checklist for reading aloud. Ask the students to experiment with a partner, trying out what it's like when you don't follow the instructions in the checklist.

3   Divide the class into pairs, and give each partner one story. Tell them they have ten minutes to read through the story and prepare to read it aloud.

4   After ten minutes, ask partners to read their stories. As they listen, partners should use the checklist, and note down what their partner does well, and what they need to improve.

9.3 Building sounds: story orchestra

Level   Elementary and above

Any story can be used for this activity, to match the level of your class.

Time   20 minutes

Aims   To mark stories for sound effects; to match text to sound effect; to focus on verbs for sounds.

Preparation

The students will need to become very familiar with the story you choose for this activity.

You could either:

• photocopy the text of the story above, or any other story from this book or elsewhere, OR

• use a story that the students know already, one that can be told without a text.

Procedure

1   Ask the students to think about the 'sound effects' that they as a class would be able to make to illustrate a story or play. Draw up their ideas on the blackboard and try them out. With an elementary class, the discussion could be in the mother tongue, but your notes of their ideas could be in English. Below is a possible list:

clap	knock on the table
stamp	hammer the table with a fist
hiss	whistle
whisper	musical instruments: drums, whistles, bells
squeak	exclamations: Oooh! Aaah!
scratch	

2   Introduce the story you have chosen to the class. Remind the students of the details of the story or read the new story you have given them.

3   Now divide the class into groups of three or four. Ask each group to

decide where in the story it would be interesting or helpful to introduce sounds: for example, clapping, stamping, whispering, or thumping. They should nominate one person to write director's notes, with a list of the 'sound effects' and the event/moment in the story.

4 Ask them to practise telling the story aloud, making the noises for themselves at each point they have marked.

5 After ten minutes, invite each group to 'perform' their story. Ask each group to listen and note down the effects they liked.

6 Ask the class to choose the noises they thought were most effective.

Devise a class version of the notes, and set the story up with the whole class performing the noise effects.

Follow-up

For homework, ask your students to select any story they have written in your classes, or which they would like to retell.

Ask them to follow the same procedure and to mark their story for sound effects.

In the next lesson, they can 'teach' the sounds to the class and perform the story.

9.4 Finding voices

With practice, it is possible to play all the parts in your story convincingly: the men, women, wicked characters, heroes and heroines.

Level Elementary and above

Time 10 minutes

Aim To play all the parts, changing voice to match character and mood; to look at the effect of stress patterns and intonation on mood and meaning; to focus on adverbs of manner.

Preparation

Here are four ways you can change your voice:

• breath: the amount of breath you use
• speed: talking very fast or very slowly
• pitch: talking very high or very low
• volume: talking very loud or very quiet.

Here are some other tips on ways to alter your voice:

Ways of speaking: further tips for the teacher

- Pleading: make long vowels even longer: Pleeeeeeease!
- Angry: spit out the words with plosive consonants: /b/, /p/: a PiPe! Is that all?!
- Scolding, angry: separate out each word, with unusually long pauses between each.
- You. Must. Pay. Me. Or. You. Will. Be. Sorry.
- Excited: generate long sentences with and ... and ... and ... clauses, and say them very, very quickly.
- Tired or drunk: make vowel sounds shorter and slur your words.
- Nasty and evil: make sounds from the back of the throat by pulling back the tongue. This gives the effect of generating a cracking, coughing sound.
- Sound like a man (if you are a woman): lower the pitch of your voice by pulling back the tongue and making sounds further down the throat. Practise sounding aaaaa, so it can be felt vibrating at the base of the neck.
- Sound like a woman (if you are a man): raise the pitch of your voice by pushing the tongue forward and making sounds further up the throat.

1 Draw the chart below on the blackboard. Choose examples that your class will understand.

Mood	Ways of speaking
excited	very quickly
sad	quietly, slowly
tired	slowly, with long yawns
shy	very quietly
frightened	fast, breathless
angry	very loud, words separated
sympathetic and kind	softly
threatening	with a nasty cackle or crack, nasty cackling laughter
amused	holding back laughter, voice begins to crack slightly

2 Ask your class if they can add any other suggestions.

3 Here are some lines from the story at the beginning of the chapter. Read these aloud to the students or write them on the blackboard.
- Pay me for my services!

• Pay you?! All you brought with you was a pipe!

Ask your class to work in groups of two and three. Their task is to say the lines to one another, using different 'ways of speaking' listed on the blackboard.

Pay me for my services! feeling shy, tired, angry, excited

Ask them to say the two lines to one another in four ways, changing the mood and tone each time.

4 Now ask the students to work with a line from a story of their own, or one they want to tell the class.

Come here, my dear.
Oh Grandmother, what big teeth you have!

Ask partner A to try out their story line, using different ways of speaking.

Partner B must guess the mood and the situation that caused it.
• You are very pleased, because you like Grandma's dentist.
• You are very nasty and about to kill Grandma with a gun hidden in your coat.
• You are amazed. You have just realized Grandma is really made of plastic.

If the mood is not clear, partner A should exaggerate the way of speaking until it is clear.

Then the partners should reverse roles, and partner B should try out the activity using another story line.

5 Here is an additional, or alternative, step to 3 above.

PARTNER A: give partner B an instruction for how to say the line and why.
PARTNER B: follow your partner's instructions until he/she is satisfied that the mood has been conveyed.

Then reverse roles.

Variation

The story lines can also be practised:
• to show the effect of different kinds of punctuation
• to show the effect of stress on different parts of the sentence:

Where can I find the pot of *gold*? (not the pot of vegetable soup)
Where can *I* find the pot of gold? (and not all my friends, who are also looking for it)

Follow-up

If your students have stories they want to tell one another, ask them for homework to return to these, and mark each line of speech with 'director's notes' to suggest how the line should be read aloud or performed.

In a later lesson, they could read their story aloud, following their own director's notes.

9.5 Mime a conversation

Level Elementary and above

Time 20 minutes

Aims To match gestures to specific language functions such as stopping, inviting; to look at body language.

Procedure

1 Write the following phrases on the board. Ask the students to suggest how they would 'say' these phrases with gestures instead of words. Is there a typical gesture in their cultures? Do they have a personal gesture for each of these?

Ask them to work in groups, sharing the gestures for each phrase. Suggest that students make their gestures bigger and more exaggerated, in order to convey their meaning. Below are examples of gestures often used to express these statements.

Stop!   Waiter, I'd like to pay the bill.
Come here!   Taxi!
Stop that behaviour   Get out of here!
   immediately.   Sit down.
Mm, he's a bit crazy.   No! I will NOT do that!
It's a secret.

Photocopiable © Oxford University Press

2   After five minutes, bring all the groups together. Invite each group to 'perform' one of the phrases. The other groups must guess what each gesture means. The group with the most correct guesses is the winner.

Follow-up

As a follow-up, students can plan a whole conversation, using mime and gesture only. Invite them to 'perform' this to the class. The class can 'write the script' as they watch.

When the students have worked with this activity, ask them to return to a story they have read or written, and identify places in the story where mime and gesture would work well. Practise 'telling' the story in small groups, using these mimes and movements.

9.6 Mime a thought

Level Elementary and above

Time 20 minutes

Aims To match adverbs of behaviour and mime; to look at language to describe behaviour; to study body language for expressing feelings and thoughts.

Preparation

You will need four blank labels for each student. You can ask the students to make these for themselves, by dividing sheets of blank A4 paper into four, when you reach step 4 below.

Procedure

1   Choose five or six adverbs that suit the level of your students and write them on the blackboard. Below are some examples for upper-intermediate to proficiency-level learners.

vainly   lovingly   crazily   angrily   seductively

Ask the students what all these words have in common. (They are all adverbs of manner.)

Invite them to add to the list.

2   Now ask the learners to choose one of the 'behaviours' from the list and mime it to their partner. Can the partner guess which behaviour they have chosen? Ask them to refine and exaggerate their 'mime' so the behaviour becomes absolutely clear.

3   After five minutes, explain that the students are now going to write director's notes for each behaviour. Ask them to work with a partner, and choose four adverbs of manner. For each one, ask them to list at least three ways to 'act'. They should write their ideas on a label, using one label for each adverb.

How to act vainly	How to act lovingly
play with your hair keep adjusting your clothes keep looking in the mirror	sit very close listen with rapt attention hold eye contact smile dreamily

How to act crazily	How to act angrily
laugh wildly and for no reason smile vacantly look into the far distance	stamp your feet grind your teeth clench your fists.

4   After ten minutes, collect up all the descriptions and shuffle them. Hand out a new description for each group. The group must now use the description to act out the behaviour.

Ask them to rehearse this, ready for a competition. If they disagree with the instructions on the label, they should change or edit it.

5   After five minutes, ask each pair to 'act' their behaviour. The pair with the most correct guesses is the winner.

Follow-up

Ask the learners now to return to the story at the beginning of this chapter, or another story of their choice, and write notes for mimes, movements and gestures.
They could also replace words and phrases in the story with mimes.

In the next lesson, they could tell their stories in small groups, using the mimes they have selected.

9.7 Choruses and cascades

This is one of the rare occasions where the larger the class is, the more possibilities there are. A large class can create 'instant' and exciting theatre by generating many different sound patterns.

Level   Elementary and above

Time   20 minutes

Aims   To look at the different effects of words and sounds in chorus; to practise choral reading; to study rhythm and pace in speaking aloud.

Ways of dividing the class

In two halves:
for blocks of sound:
front/back, right side/left side
for overlap and 'cacophony' of sound:
divide the class into pairs
all partner As in the room
make sound A
all partner Bs in the room
make sound B.

In lines/waves:
to create a wave effect, divide the class into groups:
• rows of five to ten, from the front to the back of the room
• interlocking circles, with three or four in each circle, using an open space in the classroom.

To create a 'dialogue' effect:
groups of four or five, one group in each corner of the room
• Contrast the voice of an individual storyteller/character with choral voices
• Contrast choral voices in one part of the room with voices in another part
• Contrast a large chorus with a small one
• Contrast the groups all saying the same thing with the groups all saying different things
• Contrast the groups speaking in strict turns with the groups overlapping with one another.

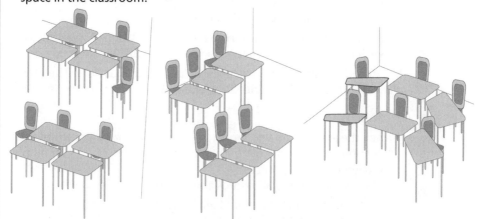

Procedure

1   Ask the students to think about 'crowd scenes' in stories they have read, heard, seen, or written.
   • *What does the crowd do?*
   • *What does the crowd say?*
   • *What does the crowd represent?* (for more advanced groups)

2   Explain that they are going to practise being the crowd in a story they all know. The activity below is based on the Pied Piper, but can be used with any story of your choice.

   Ask them to think about the story and where/when crowds might appear:
   • when the people beg the town council to get rid of the rats
   • when the people arrive to watch the rat-catcher lead the rats away
   • when the head of the town council refuses to pay the rat-catcher
   • when the rat-catcher leads the children away.

3   For each of these 'crowd' moments, ask them to suggest: language/words/phrases:

- The rats! Get rid of the rats! Get rid of the rats!
- Lead them away! Away ! Away ! Away!

4   Try out different ways of dividing up your group, depending on their size and the flexibility of the room space. Use different techniques to practise the 'crowd' voices:

- They can overlap and form a cacophony building up: *Rats/Rats/Rats*
- They can have a dialogue, shouting from opposite sides of the room:
  Send them away! Who? The rats! Send them away! Who?

Follow-up

Ask the learners to return to their own stories and plan choral voices for all the class to join in. They can edit and annotate their own text, and try it out with a small group to see if it works well.

9.8 Turning story into theatre: props and music

Level   Elementary and above

Time   Class preparation: 20 minutes

Classroom theatre: full lesson

Aims   To turn a story into a performance or piece of classroom theatre.

Procedure

1   Tell or read the Pied Piper story or another of your choice. The learners could also tell their own stories, and they could be the teacher in this activity. When the story is finished, ask the students if they have enjoyed it and elicit any first thoughts, ideas, and impressions.

2   Now explain that the learners are all going to be involved in telling the story and that the story is going to be turned into a mini-performance. The chart below lists some specific ways this might be done. Which suggestions do your learners think would work? Do they have any further suggestions?

Ask the learners to discuss these suggestions in groups of four or five.

If they like a particular idea, ask them to suggest exactly how, and by whom, it can be carried out.

Below is an illustration of what might be generated by this discussion, what the different possibilities are, and how these might be applied to the story of the Pied Piper.

Turning story into theatre: Pied Piper

Music:
- musical instruments: drums, pipes, guitar
- sing, whistle or hum a song
- tape or CD of music
- one student whistling the Pied Piper's tune: or an actual pipe or flute

Objects:
- items of clothing: gloves, hat, boots
- household objects: a saucepan, a cooking spoon
- masks: complete face masks, eye masks
- balloons: for birds, aeroplanes, clouds, ideas of flying
- sheets, ribbons and scarves: can be moved in different shapes to suggest wind, clouds, sea, rain
- cardboard sheets: when moved, sound like waves and wind
- black scarves for every student to suggest the running of the rats
- coloured ribbons for every student to suggest the running of the children

Home-made props:
- puppets made from gloves or paper bags
- wooden spoons with painted faces
- silhouettes cut out of black paper and brightly lit, behind a white sheet

People as props:
- hands and fingers as shadows projected onto a white sheet
- people making shapes to suggest buildings, trees, doorways

3 When each group has made suggestions, bring the class together. Come to an agreement about which ideas should be used, and who should do what.

Invite volunteers to carry out each suggestion and agree on a date for all of the 'props' to be brought in.

4 Practise the story with the 'props' as agreed in the working plan. Work out whether the plan needs to be changed, modified or adapted, or whether further props might be needed.

Very few, and simple props are more effective than complex or elaborate ones; so encourage the students to be selective and minimal in their choice. The story will speak for itself.

If possible, the story can now be performed to other groups so they too can experience the excitement of performed story.

9.9 Editing for performance

Level   Intermediate and above

Time   40 minutes

Aims   To practise editing for performance.

Preparation

Make copies of the Pied Piper of Hamelin story at the start of this chapter.

Procedure

1   Ask the learners to work in groups of three and four. Give each group a copy of the Pied Piper story.

2   Ask the students to annotate the story as a team of directors planning a theatre performance of the story. The instructions should all be possible for the class to carry out, using objects, props, and people available in your school. Notes for each of the following need to be added to the text:

   - sound effects, including instructions for musicians
   - instructions for the performers about mood, voice, behaviour
   - instructions for the props team, about objects, scenery, props that need to be made.

3   After 20 minutes, or when you feel the groups have completed their task, ask groups to join with one another in 'editing teams' of six to eight. Ask them to compare their ideas and formulate a joint set of directors' notes, using the best ideas from both groups.

Follow-up

Ask the teams to prepare a mini-performance of their story to perform to the class in the next lesson (or whenever is practical).

Variation

This activity can be tried out with any story your learners are familiar with, including those they have written themselves. You can collect and file their annotated stories, and use them as examples with future classes.

10

Publishing stories

This chapter helps the storywriter to edit both for clarity of language, and for vividness and effectiveness of the story. It works both with fluency of ideas, and with accuracy of expression. Ideally in a story, the language will be bright and vivid where the writer chooses, mysterious and ambiguous where he or she chooses. The language will not distract us by being inaccurate or clumsy, but will read smoothly so the reader hardly notices it is there. These activities and checklists will help the storyteller to edit a story so it is ready to go public, checking whether the ideas in the writer's head really communicate themselves to the outside world, and helping the writer to refine, edit, and correct language so it makes a smooth bridge between the writer and the story s/he wishes to tell.

In this chapter, the following story will be used as an example. The underlined words and sentences are those that could be omitted or changed for a less advanced class.

The ghost pianist

Magda's first day in her new house was very busy. <u>She worked very hard, unpacking boxes and moving furniture</u>. She decided to put her piano in the room at the back of the house. It was a <u>strange, dusty</u> room with a wooden floor. The door <u>creaked</u> and the windows had not been cleaned for years.

That night, Magda heard a strange noise: it was a *plink plonk, plink plonk*. 'I must be dreaming,' Magda thought. 'Can it be true? Someone is playing the piano!' She <u>crept</u> downstairs to the room with the piano. Nothing was there, nothing at all.

The next night, it happened again. *Plink plink plonk*. For three nights the midnight pianist came to the house and played <u>a few tuneless notes</u>, then disappeared <u>without a trace</u>.

On the fourth night, Magda waited in the corner of the room. At midnight, there was a <u>scratching</u> at the door. Then a black paw appeared under the crack, two black ears, two bright green eyes, and then a whole huge <u>tom</u>cat pushed itself under the door. <u>With one proud leap,</u> it jumped onto the piano, its tail swinging from side to side and began its <u>ghostly tune</u>: *plink plonk plink plink plonk*.

> After two or three journeys up and down the keyboard, it jumped back to the floor, washed its paws with a long pink tongue, then squeezed under the door and back out <u>into the darkness.</u>

10.1 Editing for connections between ideas

Level Intermediate and above

Time 40 minutes

Aims To look at ways in which ideas in a text are connected; to edit a story for connections between ideas.

Preparation

Make copies of one story for each student in your class. You could use the story at the start of this chapter, or any other story in this book, and adapt it to suit your students' level.

Ask the learners to bring to the lesson a story they have written.

Procedure

1 Select three disconnected sentences from different parts of the story you have chosen. Write these on the board. Below is an example from *The ghost pianist*.

   i She worked very hard, unpacking boxes and moving furniture.
   ii It was a strange, dusty room with a wooden floor.
   iii The next night, it happened again.

2 Ask the students to look at the three sentences on the board, and ask them:
   * *Are these sentences connected?*
   * *Do these three sentences make sense?*
   * *Why? Or why not?*

   Below are some possible answers. Write these on the board.
   The sentences do not connect because:
   * We don't know who 'she' is in sentence i.
   * We don't know what 'it' refers to in sentence iii.
   * We don't know what 'again' refers to in sentence iii.
   * 'The next night' suggests that other nights have been mentioned earlier, but we know nothing about these.

3 Now hand out the full text of the story. Ask the learners to read the story, and see what information they now have to help them understand the meaning of the three sentences.
   * 'She' is Magda, the main character in the story. The story is about **her** house and **her** piano.
   * The 'furniture' in sentence i includes '*her piano*'.

- 'It' in sentence ii refers to 'the room at the back of the house', where Magda puts her piano. The 'it' joins the second and third sentences in the full story.
- 'It' in sentence iii refers to the sound of a ghostly pianist playing in the middle of the night. The 'it' refers to everything described in paragraph 3 of the full story.
- 'Again' refers to the events in paragraph 3 of the full story.
- 'The next night' is the second night that Magda hears the ghost pianist. One earlier night has already been referred to.

4 Elicit from your learners 'how to link ideas together', based on what they have learnt about the three sentences. There are some examples on the next page.

Editing for connections between ideas

- Pronouns, such as *it, she, he*, can link sentences together.
- Pronouns can refer back to a single word or idea in the sentence before.
- *It* can refer back to a whole paragraph or set of ideas.
- Adverbs such as *again, next* refer the reader to what has gone before.
- Adverbs of time mark the sequence/timing/stages in a story: *then, after that, the next night, the first time/fourth time*.
- The first time a character appears, it is usual to use their name. Afterwards, they can be referred to as *he/she*.
- Using different words to describe the same object/person connects ideas: for example: *furniture, her piano, the keyboard, notes*.
- You can also refer to something by describing its parts: for example: *paw, ears, green eyes, pink tongue = cat*.
- The first time a new idea is introduced, you can use the indefinite article *a*; the second time it can be referred to using the definite article *the*: for example, a wooden floor/the floor; a huge tomcat/the cat.

Photocopiable © Oxford University Press

5 When you have discussed all the above 'connecting' techniques with your class, ask your learners to work with a partner, and look at their own story or piece of writing.

Ask the learners to check the 'connecting techniques' in their own and their partner's work, using the checklist you have drawn up together.

- Does the story read as clear and connected?
- Is there a variety of techniques to connect the ideas?
- Do any corrections or additions need to be made?

Follow-up

Once you have worked through this activity, and learners are familiar with the checklist, they can use it for self-correction after completing a story or piece of writing.

10.2 Editing for punctuation

Level Pre-intermediate and above

Time 40 minutes

Aims To practise punctuation for making sense of a text; to edit a story for punctuation.

Preparation

Select one of the stories in this book, or any other story, that matches the level and interests of your learner. Write it out, omitting all the punctuation marks, and make copies for all your learners.

Procedure

1 Give your students a copy of your chosen story, without punctuation marks.

Ask them to look through the story and tell you:

- *What is wrong with the way the story is written?*
- *Can you make sense of the story? Why, or why not?*
- *What would help you?*

2 Ask your learners to suggest the punctuation that is missing. Draw up with them a checklist of ideas, and write these on the board for reference. The list below is an example.

Editing for punctuation

To make sense of a story/text we need:

- full stops and capital letters to show the ends of sentences
- commas to divide up phrases or words in a list
- apostrophes (') to show possession (for example, Magda's house)
- apostrophes (') to show a missing letter (for example, it's = it is)
- inverted commas ('.......,') to show direct speech or thoughts
- a colon: to introduce a list
- capital letters to show the names of people and places
- paragraphs to show the start of a new idea, situation, or event
- question marks for questions.

Photocopiable © Oxford University Press

3   Ask your learners now to work with a partner and use this checklist to edit and correct the story.

4   After ten minutes, hand out the correct version of the story. Ask your learners to compare their own versions and the original one, and notice any differences.

They might suggest:

- exclamations to show emphasis
- indented lines to show the start of a paragraph (leaving an empty line is another possibility).

Follow-up

Ask your learners to use this checklist to correct the punctuation in a story or piece of writing of their own.

Variations

If you would like to focus on one particular aspect of punctuation, you could delete only that in the story you have chosen.
For example, in *The ghost pianist*, you could focus only on the beginnings and endings of sentences, by omitting all the full stops and capital letters.

Comments

Typical punctuation errors you may wish to focus on are apostrophes. Apostrophes should be used only where a letter is omitted, or to show possession.
They are often used in error with the plural *-s* ending.

For example:

- the cats paw's: incorrect
- the cat's paws: correct.

10.3 Editing for form and function

Level Pre-intermediate and above

Time 20 minutes

Aims To check the way time is referred to in a story; to check that each sentence has a finite verb; to edit for variety of verb forms.

Preparation

Bring copies of a story that matches the level and interests of your class. The examples below are based on *The ghost pianist* (at the start of this chapter).

You will need a set of whiteboard pens or sticks of chalk, so each group can write on the board.

Procedure

1   Give the learners copies of the story you have chosen. Ask them to read the story and underline all the **verbs** they can find.

2 After five minutes, ask the students to count how many verbs they have underlined, and make a quick count. *How many of you found more than ten? More than five?*

3 With a more advanced class you might want to discuss:
  • How did you decide what a verb was?
  • What was included in the verb? The pronoun/subject? The preposition that followed? The auxiliary and participles?
  • Did you choose only verbs with a subject? Only verbs with a time reference? Only verbs in complete sentences? (finite verbs?)

4 Now ask the learners to work in groups. Allocate to each group one of the boxes in the board chart below, depending on the level of your group. Ask each group to collect and write into the box all the verbs in the story that match the title of the box.

The examples come from *The ghost pianist*.

Group A:	Group B:	Group C:
Verbs describing past time	Modal verbs (might, may, should, must)	Verbs that do not describe time clearly (non-finite verbs)
was scratching	I must be dreaming	unpacking
was swinging	Can it be true?	moving
jumped		swinging
washed		
pushed		
licked		
had not been cleaned		

Group D:	Group E:
Verbs describing present time	Verbs describing future time *
is playing	

* *The ghost pianist* does not include verbs in the future. Include this box only when there are examples in the story you have chosen.

5 After ten minutes ask each group to elect a group representative. Give each representative a stick of chalk or a whiteboard pen and ask them to write their group list onto the blackboard.

6 Now you have a full list from each group, ask the class to review the chart.
  • Is each verb in the correct place? Do any corrections or changes need to be made?
  • In how many different ways is past time referred to? Present time? Future time?
  • In what places in the sentence can you find verbs with an -*ing* ending or an -*ed* ending? (for example, as a noun: 'a scratching' or as a phrase describing a noun: 'its tail swinging')

7 Using the chart, draw up with your learners an editing checklist for verbs in a story.

There is a possible list on the next page

Editing for variety of verb form and function

To make a story interesting, include a variety of verb forms and functions:

Past time can be referred to in several ways:

- Someone <u>was playing</u> the piano (past progressive or continuous)
- The windows <u>had not been cleaned</u> for years (past perfect/passive voice)
- It <u>happened</u> again (simple past).

Present time/tense can make a story vivid and immediate. Characters in the story can talk in the present tense.

Modal verbs can introduce a feeling of suspense or speculation.

<u>Can</u> it be true?! I <u>must be dreaming</u>!

Non-finite verbs ending with -ing can make descriptions vivid and dynamic:

- its tail <u>swinging</u> from side to side.

Verbs describing actions are more interesting than verbs with no movement, such as *to be* and *to have*:

- pushed, jumped, washed, squeezed

Dynamic verbs like these **make something happen.**

Photocopiable © Oxford University Press

8 Now ask the learners to use this editing checklist to find the verbs in their own story.

- Have you used a variety of verb forms to make your story interesting?
- Could you edit the verb forms to make your story more vivid?

Variations

This activity can be adapted to match any aspect of verbs you wish to practise with your group. Other aspects of verbs include:

- passive mood: *the windows had not been cleaned for years*
- transitive verbs: verbs with an object, such as *the tomcat washed its paws*
- intransitive verbs: verbs without an object, which are either complete on their own, or need to be followed by a preposition: *it leapt onto the piano* (not *it leapt the piano*).
- verbs describing the senses: *hear, see, smell, touch, taste*
- present tense verbs in the third person singular: do they have the -s ending?

10.4 Editing for vocabulary: synonym race

Level Pre-intermediate and above

Time 20 minutes

Aims To practise the use of synonyms in a story; to edit stories for richness and variety of vocabulary.

Preparation

Bring a set of dictionaries or thesauri, if that is possible. Learners should bring to this lesson a copy of a story or piece of writing of their own.

Procedure

1 Read or tell your learners *The ghost pianist* story (at the start of this chapter). Ask them to listen and to write down at least three ways the cat is referred to in the story.

Below is a list:

black (furry, hairy) paws	two black ears
green eyes	long pink tongue
swinging tail	huge tomcat

With more advanced learners, you could suggest a discussion:

Do you think this list of words is more or less interesting than simply writing 'the cat/the cat/the cat'? Why? Or why not?

Elicit from your learners other ways they could describe the cat in the story, and write these on the blackboard.

2 Now divide your learners into teams of four and five. Explain they are going to play a synonym race. They must write down as many words or phrases as they can in two minutes, referring to a keyword that you will allocate.

They can use dictionaries and thesauri to help them, if these are available in class.

Allocate one keyword that belongs to the story you have read to them. For *The ghost pianist*, for example:

the piano: the musical instrument, the keys, the keyboard, the notes, the hammers, the wooden case, shining white teeth, etc.

3 After two minutes, stop the class and ask each group to count their examples. Ask them to read their lists aloud and 'vote' on whether each word is a good alternative for the 'keyword'. The winner is the group with the most words voted as 'good'.

Write on the blackboard all the words that are voted as good alternatives.

4 Use the blackboard list to elicit a discussion:

- How does each word connect with the original keyword?
- What can we do in a story, instead of using the same word twice?

With the group, draw up a checklist of possibilities. Below is an example:

Editing for vocabulary checklist

Instead of using the same word twice:

- use a different word altogether that means the same (a synonym)
- refer to a part only (the paws/ears of the cat)
- make a word more specific (tomcat instead of cat)
- make a word more general (musical instrument instead of piano)
- use a metaphor for the object (shining white teeth for the piano keyboard)
- change the 'feeling' of the word (from positive to negative or vice versa).

Follow-up

Now ask the learners to look again at a story of their own. Ask them to find one word in their story that they repeat more than three times.

Ask them to use a dictionary or thesaurus to find words that they could use as an alternative, and to include these words in their story.

Variations

Words that are typically used too often in stories are:

nice
beautiful
say
reply.

1 Divide your class into four groups and give each group one of the 'headwords' listed above.

Ask each group to find as many synonyms for their headword as possible in five minutes.

If dictionaries or thesauri are available, encourage your learners to use them.

2 After five minutes, stop the groups and ask them to count the number of synonyms they have found. The winning group, with the most number of words, should read out their list.

For example:

say: *tell, utter, repeat, state, confirm, agree, shout, argue, comment*

3 Now ask each group to look at the words in the lists they have prepared, and think of a context for each of the words. Could they use all the words interchangeably? How do the words differ? Could they use all the words in their story?

10.5 Editing for stylistic variety: Alphonse's story

Level Intermediate and above

Time 20 minutes

Aims To edit stories for variety of sentence types; to include in stories both complex and simple sentences; to include in stories both coordinate and subordinate clauses.

Preparation

Choose a story that matches the level and interests of your class. Rewrite the story so it contains only short, simple sentences. Below is an example.

Make copies of the story for each learner.

Alphonse's story

Alphonse was very poor. He wanted to make money quickly. He had an idea. He picked lots of grapes and made a very nice juice. He tasted the juice to see if it was nice. It was so nice that he began to sing songs very loudly. He sang so loudly that his family had to lock him in the washroom at the back of the house. All day people came to buy the juice. Everyone wanted to buy some. All day, the loud songs came from the washroom. At last he became tired. He stopped singing. They let him out of the washroom. They said, 'We have sold all the juice! Everyone loves it! We are rich!'

'Hooray!' he said. 'Let's celebrate!' So he poured himself a glass of juice. Then he poured another. Then another. Soon he was back again, locked in the washroom.

'Too much of a good thing is a bad thing,' his wife said through the door of the washroom.

'Too much of a good thing is an even better thing,' he replied.

Photocopiable © Oxford University Press

Procedure

1 Write on the board the first two sentences of your story. Below is an example, taken from *Alphonse's story*.

Example Alphonse was very poor. He wanted to make money quickly.

2 Ask your class to suggest different ways the two sentences could be joined. Explain they can move the words around in any way they like, and add any words or phrases they like to join the sentences.

Examples of joining words are given on the next page.

Below are some possibilities.

Joining words

because	Alphonse wanted to make money quickly, because he was very poor.
although	Although he was very poor, Alphonse wanted to make money quickly.
so (as a joining word)	Alphonse was very poor, so he wanted to make money quickly.
so (as an adverb)	Alphonse was so poor, he wanted to make money quickly.
but	Alphonse wanted to make money quickly, but he was very poor.
and	Alphonse was very poor, and he wanted to make money quickly.

Photocopiable © Oxford University Press

3 Ask your learners to vote on which version they like best. Ask them to explain their choice briefly. Their choice could be based on a preference for:

- long or short sentences
- how sentences are joined: both sentences are equal (joined by and/or); one sentence is more important than the other
- the word order of sentences: which idea is put first? The idea that comes first is often the one with the most emphasis.

4 Now explain that they will be editing the story (their own and the stories of others) so the sentences are varied:

- in the way they are joined: using different joining words
- in length: some short, some long
- in the word order.

Ask them to suggest ways that this can be done and then introduce the checklist on the next page. You could expand this checklist with the learners' own ideas.

5 Ask the learners to work in groups of two and three. Their task is to make the sentences in the story more interesting, by varying them in all the ways suggested above.

6 After ten minutes, ask each group to join with another and read out their new story versions. Notice the similarities and differences between their two versions and choose which features they like best.

7 Either for homework, or in class if there is time, ask the learners to edit their own stories for variety in sentence length, type, and word order.

Editing for stylistic variety

Ways of joining sentences:

- cause and effect: *because, as a result, so, therefore*
- contrast: *but, although, however*
- joining equal sentences: (coordination): *and, or*
- consecutive time: *when, while.*

Ways of varying sentence length:

Short sentences:

- exclamations : Help!
- short questions: What?! So what?!
- sentences with one main verb only: Alphonse's family was very poor.

Long sentences: sentences with more than one main verb. These sentences can be joined in all the ways listed above.

Ways of varying word order:

The following information can come at the beginning of the sentence:

- the subject: *Alphonse/he*
- a phrase describing time: *at last, soon, all day*
- a phrase describing place: *in the washroom, on the table, in the bottle*
- new information: *for example, the name of the character, Alphonse*
- a pronoun: *he, she, it*
- an adverb: *happily, unfortunately*: Unfortunately, he sang so loudly his family had to lock him in the washroom.

Photocopiable © Oxford University Press

Follow-up

When the learners have finished editing their own stories for sentence variety, ask them to exchange with a partner. They should read one another's stories, and mark with a ✓ each time the sentences have been made interesting and varied.

10.6 Editing for story ideas: story interviews

Level Intermediate and above

The questions in the checklist can be adapted for pre intermediate level.

Time 20 minutes

Aims To make the main story idea clear; to edit story for development and key story ingredients.

Preparation

Make copies of the editing checklist on p. 155 for each student. Adapt the questions in the checklist to suit the language level of your students.

Ask the learners to bring a story of their own to the class. This activity is most useful once students have already planned and begun to work on their own stories.

Procedure

1 Explain to the learners they are going to act as story editors for one another. Their job is to decide whether their partner's story is ready for publication/performance by your publishing/theatre company. (You choose the context that suits your class best.)

 Elicit from the class the kind of questions they will ask one another and make a note of these questions on the board.

2 Divide your class into pairs, with one group of three if you have an uneven number. Each student will act both as interviewee, and as story editor.

 As interviewee, they must respond carefully to the editor's questions, and take notes of his/her recommendations.

 As story editors, they must interview their partner, using their own ideas, the class ideas, and the checklist below as guidelines. The editing checklist on the next page includes questions for the interviewee and a framework for offering recommendations.

3 Ask the students to work in pairs, interviewing each other and offering advice. Ask each student to make a list of recommendations for their story.

4 For homework, ask each student to build these recommendations into a new version of their story.

Variation

The editing checklist can also be used for self-editing. Ask the learners to add further questions of their own to this checklist, and to use it to edit their own work and draw up recommendations for themselves.

Editing for story ideas: story interviews

- How would you complete this sentence: *My story is about …*
- If you can't complete the sentence, can you make your story ideas clearer?
- What would you like me/the reader to remember most about your story?
- Can you tell me three ways you have made this aspect of the story memorable?
- If the answer is **no**, then use the checklists in this chapter to find at least three ways of making your story or language more vivid.
- Has anything changed between the beginning and the ending of your story?
- If the answer is **no**, then think about introducing a change, however small.
- Have we learnt something new about the main character?
- If the answer is **no**, then introduce more information about the main character.
- What would you like me to remember about the setting of the story? What can the reader see/smell/touch/hear?
- If you're not sure, think about how you could create a memorable setting.
- Why do you think I should read your story? What makes it special, unusual, or interesting?
- If you're not sure, think about changing the characters, plot, setting, or topic so you are convinced that it is saying something new and interesting.

Photocopiable © Oxford University Press

10.7 Editing for characterization

Level Intermediate and above

The questions in the checklist can be adapted for pre-intermediate level.

Time 20 minutes

Aims To consider the techniques for making characters vivid; to edit a story for characterization.

Preparation

Make copies of the editing checklist on page 156 for each student. Adapt the questions in the checklist to suit the language level of your learners.

Ask the learners to bring a story of their own to the class. This activity is most useful once the students have already written the first version of their own stories.

Procedure

1   Explain to the learners that they are going to edit their own work to see whether their character is vivid, interesting, and convincing. Elicit from the class the ways in which characters can be made vivid in a story, and make a note of these on the board.

2   Ask the students to work on their own with the first draft of their story. They should look through each of the questions in the checklist on the next page, and make a list of recommendations for changing and developing their character.

Editing for characterization

- Do we know the habits of your character?
- Do we know how he/she behaves and acts on a typical day?
- Do we know his/her particular qualities?
- Do any of these qualities or characteristics become a problem for your character? How? Why? With what results?
- If the answer is **no**, try to introduce some new ideas.

- Do the characters speak in your story?
- If the answer is **no**, introduce some conversation.
- Do we know what your character looks like?
- If not, introduce a memorable physical characteristic: for example, hair flopping over eyes, large ears or introduce a memorable item of clothing: for example, a yellow hat.

- Does your character change between the beginning and the end of the story?
- Do we discover new information about the character between the beginning and the end of the story?

- If there is more than one character, what is the difference between them?
- How are they related to one another? What do they think about each other?

Photocopiable © Oxford University Press

3   For homework, or in class if there is time, ask the learners to follow up their own recommendations and edit their story to make their character more vivid.

Variation 1

A variation of this self-editing activity is for learners to exchange stories with a partner, and work through the questions, offering recommendations to one another.

Variation 2

If the students are planning spoken story or performance, they can interview one another and give oral answers to each of the questions in the checklist.

10.8 Story editing workshop: Raoul's jungle creature

Level Intermediate and above

Time Classroom workshop: 15 minutes

Optional homework and follow-up: 30 minutes

Aims To apply the principles of expanding and developing a story.

Procedure

1 Make a copy of the two versions of the story, either on a transparency or as photocopies.

Ask the students to look at both versions and decide:

- which is the first version?
- which is the final version?
- what has changed?
- do the changes make the text clearer? More vivid? If so, why?
- can they notice specific changes that have been covered in the editing checklists in this chapter?

Below are some ideas:

- nouns and adjectives to describe the animal: *grace, agility, wonderful, marvellous*
- verbs to describe the movements of the animal: *ate, slept, washed, kept cool, kept dry*
- contrast between places is established: *a long journey through the jungle,* and *the town*
- use of synonyms: *creature, animal, beast*
- references to the time spent in the jungle: *one month,* hot weather and wet weather suggests length and changes in time
- references to the time spent retelling the story: *one hour*
- adjectives to describe Raoul's feelings about the animal: *delighted*
- conversation between the two characters
- pronouns/nouns used more clearly, so we know who 'he' is: this is confusing in the first version
- repetition of *then* in the first version is replaced by other connectors: *so, after one hour.*

2 When the students have identified the differences, ask them to make the same changes to a story of their own for homework. In the next class, they can work with a partner to compare the first version and the new version in the same way.

Version 1

One day, Raoul saw a new kind of animal in the jungle. He was interested in the animal but didn't know its name. Then he asked the philosopher if he knew its name.

The philosopher said he must go and look hard at the animal, then come and give him more information.

So Raoul went back to the forest and did look hard. When he had more information, he came back to tell the philosopher. He told the philosopher everything he had seen. So what is the animal's name? The philosopher thought for a moment, then said the name didn't matter. What Raoul knew about the animal was far more interesting.

Version 2

On his long journey through the jungle, Raoul saw a wonderful creature swinging from tree to tree. He watched the creature for many hours, and was delighted by its grace and agility. He rushed back to the town and said to the philosopher,

'Tell me the name of this marvellous creature I saw in the forest.'

The philosopher replied,

'Go back to the jungle and study the creature for one month. Then come back and tell me more about him.'

So Raoul did just that, and after a month returned to the philosopher. He told the philosopher what the creature ate and how often, where the creature slept, how the creature looked after its young and what its mate was like, how and where the creature washed, what animals the creature feared and how it protected itself, how the animal kept cool when it was very hot, how it kept dry when the rain fell. After one hour of telling the story, he said to the philosopher, 'Now tell me the name of this wonderful beast.'

'Why do you need to know its name?' the philosopher said. 'What you know is far more important.'

Variations

Alternatively, students could choose one of the story synopses from this book, and expand it using the same editing principles. *Alphonse's story* in 10.5 could also be used for this activity.

Appendices

1 Story archetypes: generative plots

Below is a list of generative plots that can be adapted to match:

- any time period
- any place
- any cultural context
- any character type: named and specific, archetypal, and mythical
- any theme: political, psychological, ecological, ethical, and philosophical.

They derive from an amalgam of many studies that have attempted to identify the universal plot types.
Some of these are listed in the reading list at the end of this section: Vladimir Propp, Ronald Tobias, Christopher Booker.

- Rags to riches: a person starts poor and becomes a great success against all odds: activity 3.7.
- Good over evil: a good person battles against evil and eventually wins (or loses).
- Small against big: the person without power or status wages a battle against a person or company with huge power: for example, the small farmer against a huge business like McDonalds.
- The guilty secret: a long-kept secret begins to reveal itself, or have an influence on events: such as the man who reveals on his wedding day that he has a mad first wife hidden in the attic (in Charlotte Brontë's *Jane Eyre*).
- The journey: activity 1.4.
- The quest: search for the ideal: as in activity 5.1, 'The shepherd and the pyramids', where the shepherd travels all the way to the pyramids to find out where the pot of gold is hidden.
- Survival: as in the Machu Pichu story, where the boy and his goat run to the top of the highest mountain to escape the floods, and take with them all the animals, birds, and insects: activity 6.5.
- The love triangle: as in Nemorino and Adina's story, Chapter 7, where Adina falls in love with Nemorino only when she sees him flirting with other girls.
- Betrayal: as in the Great Wall walk, where the two lovers fail to meet in the middle of the Great Wall of China: activity 1.4.
- Changing places: where, for example, husband and wife change places for the day: activity 1.5.

- Separation of siblings: where, for example, twins are separated at birth.
- Separation of children from parents: when Red Riding Hood leaves her mother to deliver the basket of cherries the other side of the large dark forest.
- Separation of lovers: when Odysseus leaves Penelope for many years to go to war.
- The test: where the hero/heroine must pass through a trial; for example, the story of Rumpelstiltskin, where the girl must spin straw into gold, or the story of Sheherezade, who tells the king a thrilling story every night for a thousand and one nights.
- Loss of innocence/growing up: as in the Oscar story, where Oscar must learn to 'let go' of his mother: activity 5.6.
- Crime and punishment: a story of good and evil where a person commits a crime such as murder, or a theft, is found out, and punished.
- The fatal flaw: 'traditional' flaws include hubris or pride, but there are many 'modern' fatal flaws such as addiction, jealousy, obsession, or indecision: as in the story of Dino, who cannot choose between two women: activity 5.5.

2 Character types

- The hero and heroine
- The villain
- The friend, mentor, or benefactor who gives advice
- The false friend who deceives by appearing to be a true friend, taking his/her shape or place
- The ugly duckling: a character transforms/changes, such as the ugly grey duckling who becomes a beautiful swan.
- The prodigal son: a character who has been rejected/misunderstood/cast out returns after a long absence and is accepted back into the community, as in 'Oscar's problem': activity 5.6.
- The trickster: a traditional character in many cultures, who makes mischief and survives disaster by tricking people (for example, the character of Brer Rabbit, which is derived from African-American folktales of the US South).
- The one left behind: as in the Pied Piper of Hamelin, Chapter 9, where the small boy with the bad leg is left behind after all the children have followed the piper into a cave.

3 A glossary of story types

- A soap opera: a story about the everyday lives of everyday people; soap operas do not have neat endings, just as life does not; and so can go on and on until the viewer chooses to stop viewing, or the reader to stop reading.
- A ghost story: a story about spirits, life after death, the return of spirits, former lives and reincarnation.

- A mystery story: a story with a secret or a problem to solve, such as 'The ghost pianist': Chapter 10.
- A thriller: a story designed to frighten or excite, often with unreal and fantastical events of horror, or a focus on crime, mystery, or espionage.
- A detective story: a story describing a detective's attempt to solve a crime.
- A travel story: a story about a long journey, for example, the Machu Picchu story: activity 6.5.
- A science-fiction story: a story where the limitations of our world are broken: such as travelling through time, seeing into the future, visiting other planets and universes.
- A romance: a love story, for example, 'The love potion': Chapter 7
- Myth: a story that asks questions about the world and its creation, with characters set in no specific place or time, and often with no specific names for example, 'The sky people': activity 6.4.
- Legend: a story that may relate to an actual place, event or person, and that is an attempt to explain a half understood or dimly recorded historical event for example, 'The king's dinner': activity 2.8 (the story of King Charles I's visit to Totnes in England).
- Fable: a story with a moral that is designed to teach or guide
- Fantasy: where the bizarre, strange, and wonderful all become possible.
- Graphic novels: stories told through pictures.

Further reading

Angwin, R. 2005. *Writing the Bright Moment.* Yelverton: Fire in the Head.
Writers talk about what inspires them to start writing.

Bettelheim, B. 1978. *The Uses of Enchantment.* London: Peregrine.
An analysis of the meaning of fairy tales and the psychological importance of storytelling.

Booker, C. 2004. *The Seven Basic Plots.* London, New York: Continuum.

The ER pages: http://www.extensivereading.net
Valuable resources for teachers and researchers connected with extensive reading.

ER Foundation:
Projects include stories for use in the classroom and the Language Learner literature awards.
http://www.erfoundation.org

Garvie, E. 1990. *Story as Vehicle.* Clevedon: Multilingual Matters.
An introduction to the skills and scope of using story for language acquisition in ESL contexts.

Gersie, A. and **N. King.** 1990. *Storymaking in Education and Therapy.* London: Stockholm Institute of Education Press.
Activities for building stories using archetypal myths and story themes.

Graham, C. 2000. *Jazz Chants Fairy Tales.* Oxford: Oxford University Press.
Stories for chanting and practising rhythm and intonation.

Johnstone, K. 1999. *Impro for Storytelling.* London: Faber and Faber.
The bridge between story and performance, with checklists of how to convey character and set up performance workshops.

Matthews, P. 1996. *Sing me the Creation.* Stroud: Hawthorn Press.
Ideas for developing stories using the four sentence types.

Morgan, J. and **M. Rinvolucri.** 1983. *Once upon a Time.* Cambridge: Cambridge University Press.
Story development ideas for the language classroom.

Pope, R. 1995. *Textual Intervention.* London: Routledge.
Ideas for changing one text into another, and using other texts as the starting point for stories.

Propp, V. trans. L. Scott. 1968. *The Morphology of the Folk Tale.* Texas: University of Texas Press.
An attempt to identify the universal plots found in all folktales and myths worldwide.

Rossner, R. 1988. *The Whole Story.* Harlow: Longman.
Complete stories with story development activities for the language classroom.

Story Arts online: http://www.storyarts.org
Includes story library, lesson plans, storytelling tips, and techniques.

Taylor, E. K. 2000. *Using Folktales*: Cambridge: Cambridge University Press.

Tobias, R. 1995. *Twenty Master Plots and How to Build Them.* London: Piatkus.
Plot types for storytellers.

Wajnryb, R. 2003. *Stories.* Cambridge: Cambridge University Press.

Watts, E. 2006. *Storytelling.* Oxford: Oxford University Press (Oxford Basics Series).

Wingate, J. 1990. *How to Use Storytelling in Language Teaching.* Bristol: Primary House.
Many practical ideas for using story in the language classroom.

Wright, A. 1997. *Creating Stories with Children.* Oxford: Oxford University Press (Resource Books for Teachers).
Key storytelling principles and activities that would work with both children and adult language learners.

Stories to use in class

Cambridge English Language Library
Contemporary fiction written authentically by writers for language learners, graded at 5 levels.

Dahl, R. 2001. *Revolting Rhymes*. London: Puffin. Classic fairy tales outrageously rewritten in verse.

Oxford Bookworms

Oxford English Language Library

Paran, A. and **E. Watts** (eds). 2003. *Storytelling in ELT*. Whitstable: IATEFL.
Stories written and used by teachers in their language classroom.

Pulverness, A. and **A. Moses** (eds.) 2004. *The Outsider, A Twist in the Tale, London Tales, Games People Play*. Recanati: ELI.
A series of contemporary stories commissioned from established writers, with language development activities and interviews with the authors.

Yolen, J. 1986. *Favorite Folktales from around the World*. New York: Random House.

Zipes, J. 1986. *Don't Bet on the Prince*. Aldershot: Gower Press.
Witty feminist retellings of traditional folktales from North America and England.

Stories which have inspired this book

Brontë, Charlotte. 2000 (new edition). *Jane Eyre*. Oxford: Oxford University Press. (Oxford World's Classics). Also available in a simplified ELT version (Oxford Bookworms).

Browning, Robert. 1888. *The Pied Piper of Hamelin*. London: Frederick Warne. Electronic version prepared by Jian Liu, March 1998, Reference Department, Indiana University Libraries, available at
http://www.indiana.edu/~librcsd/etext/piper/

Carver, Raymond. 1988. *Elephant and Other Stories*. London: Collins Harvill.

Daudet, Alphonse. 1947. *Lettres de mon Moulin*. London: Nelson.

Hartley, L.P. 2004 (new edition). *The Go-between*. London: Penguin (Penguin Modern Classics). Also available in a simplified ELT version (Penguin ELT).

Kafka, Franz. 2006 (new edition). *Metamorphosis* London: Penguin.

Lanchester, John. 1996. *The Debt to Pleasure*. London: Picador.

O'Connor, Frank. 1990. 'My Oedipus Complex' in *Short Stories*. London: Pan.

Index

Routes through the story activities

Story synopses

There are 25 complete mini-stories in this book. Each of them can be used in any of the activities, or simply used as a 'filler' to begin or end the lesson with a quiet listening phase. Each story synopsis takes about two minutes to read aloud, or could be recounted orally with improvisations and audience participation. (See Chapter 9 for guidance in memorizing and performing stories.)